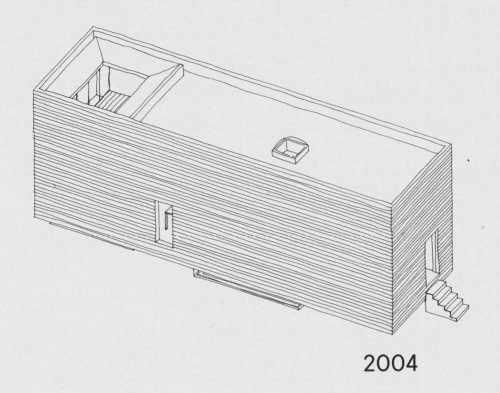

2004

2004

（2006年竣工）

2004

(Completed in 2006)

監督　YU SORA
アニメーション　YU SORA
写真　岡本充男
音楽　庄子 渉

住宅街に取り残されたクローバーの生えた地面と、その上に50cm
だけ持ち上げられた白い木箱のような家。工事のはじめから置かれ
たダイニングテーブル、浮かべられた建物に出入りする設備配管。
普通なようでどこか普通でないこの家が、YU SORAのハンドドロー
イングと、岡本充男の35mmフィルム写真で描写されます。

Director: YU SORA
Animation: YU SORA
Photo: Mitsuo Okamoto
Music: Wataru Shoji

A house that looks like a white wooden box raised only 50 centimeters
above the ground stands on a clover-covered ground that has been
left remaining in a residential area. A dining table is placed on the site at
the start of the construction, and plumbing pipes go in and out of the
floating building. YU SORA's drawings and Mitsuo Okamoto's 35-mm
film photos depict this ordinary but somewhat extraordinary house.

Film

http://hideyukinakayama.com/cinema/01

Introduction

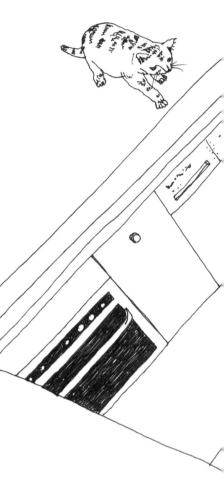

「2004」によせて
YU SORA

中山さんに初めて会ったのは2011年3月12日、震災の次の日だった。私がたまたま東京にいたその時、震災が起こった。どこか海外の知らない人たちの、自分とは関係のない話で終わったかもしれない出来事が目の前で起こった。その後も私の身近な所で、世界で、災害や事故により、突然日常を失ってしまう出来事が続いた。私にできることは、今生きている人たちがもっと日常を大切にするように、作品をつくり続けることなのではないか。そういう想いで、些細な日常生活を描いている。

中山英之展「, and then」（TOTOギャラリー・間、2019）に参加することになって、最も心が惹かれたプロジェクトは「2004」だった。家とは、どんな形の家でも人の日常が起こる舞台であり器である。人びとの生きていくことそのものであり、証しである。私は街を歩きながらいつも家を観察している。天気のいい日にベランダや庭に干されている洗濯物、鉢植え、窓から見えるカーテンや食器棚の影など、知らない人たちの似たような日常から安堵感と平和を感じる。家には建てる人がいて、住む人がいて、形を変えたりしながら世代を超え、人より長く生きる。人びとのいろんな生き方があるように、家が長く生きるなかでは、時々幸福なだけではない、いろんな時間がある。私たちは「2004」のそのいろんな時間を短い映像に収めることにした。

Thoughts on *2004*
YU SORA

I met Hideyuki Nakayama for the first time on March 12 in 2011, a day after the Tohoku Earthquake. I happened to be in Tokyo when the earthquake occurred. An incident that could have happened to strangers somewhere overseas, which would have been a story that had nothing to do with me, happened in front of my eyes. After that, various incidents that suddenly deprived people of daily life — natural disasters, accidents, and more — occurred around me one after another. What I can do is to continue to create my work that reminds those who are alive to live life to the fullest every day. I continue to depict trivial things in daily life with such thoughts in my mind.

I was invited to participate in "Hideyuki Nakayama; , and then" (TOTO GALLERY·MA, 2019). Among his projects, I was most fascinated by *2004*. A house is a stage and a vessel for people's daily life, regardless of what kind of form it may be. It is the embodiment and the proof of life itself. I always observe houses when walking on the street. Miscellaneous things in strangers' daily life just like mine — the laundry, flower pots, curtains behind the windows, shadows of cupboards in the room and so on — give me a sense of relief and peace. A house is built by people, lived in by people, reconfigured by people, and lives longer than people across the generations. A house sometimes encounters various moments that are not necessarily happy in its long life, just like how people encounter different moments in their respective lives. We decided to capture such various moments inside *2004* in a short film.

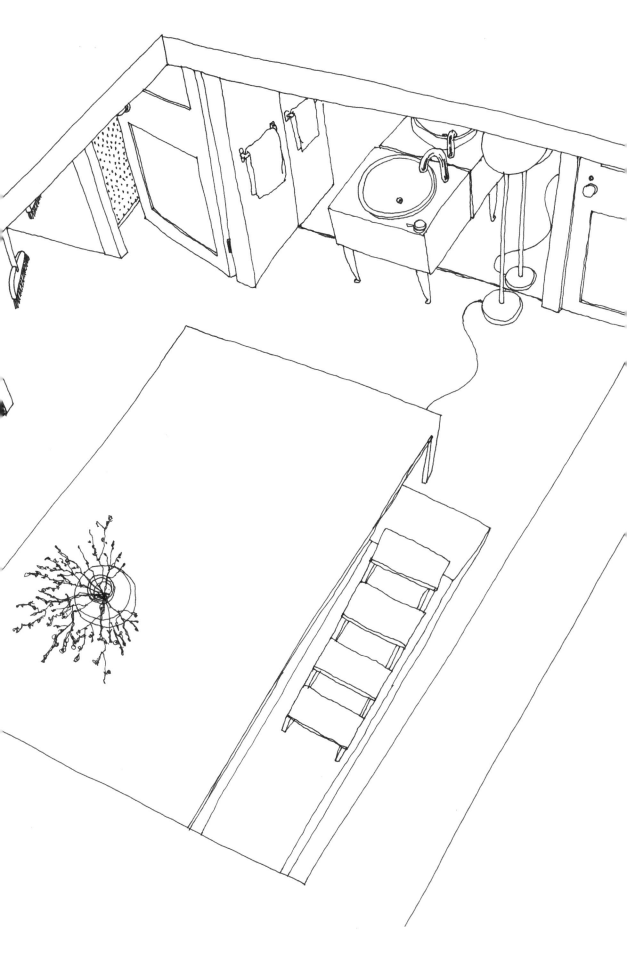

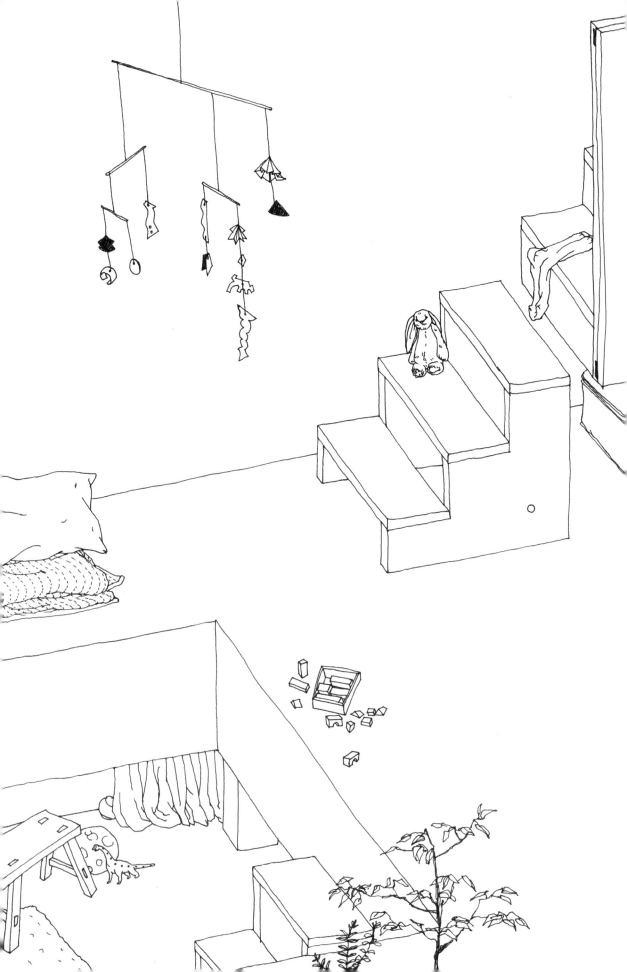

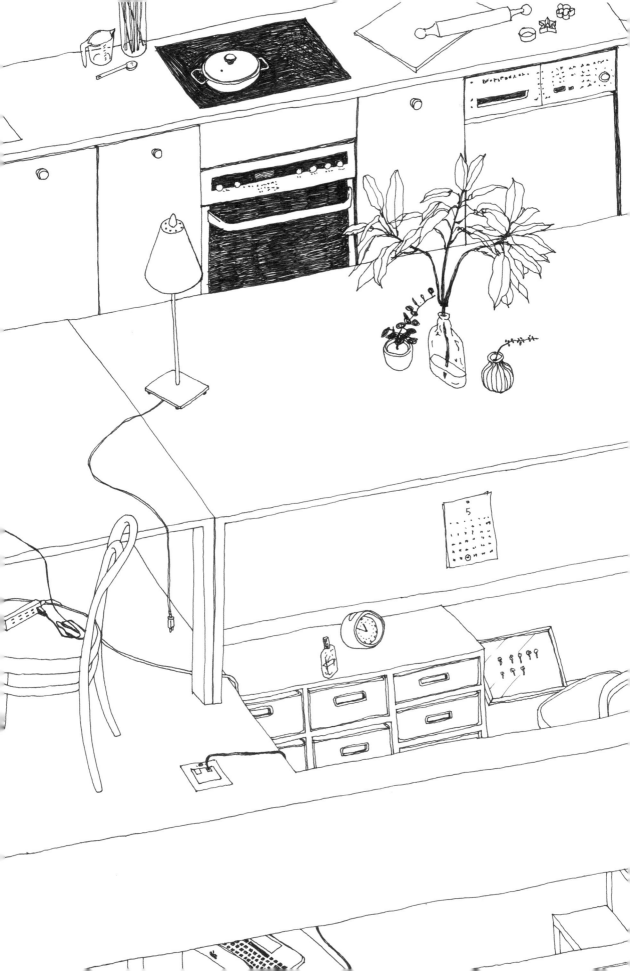

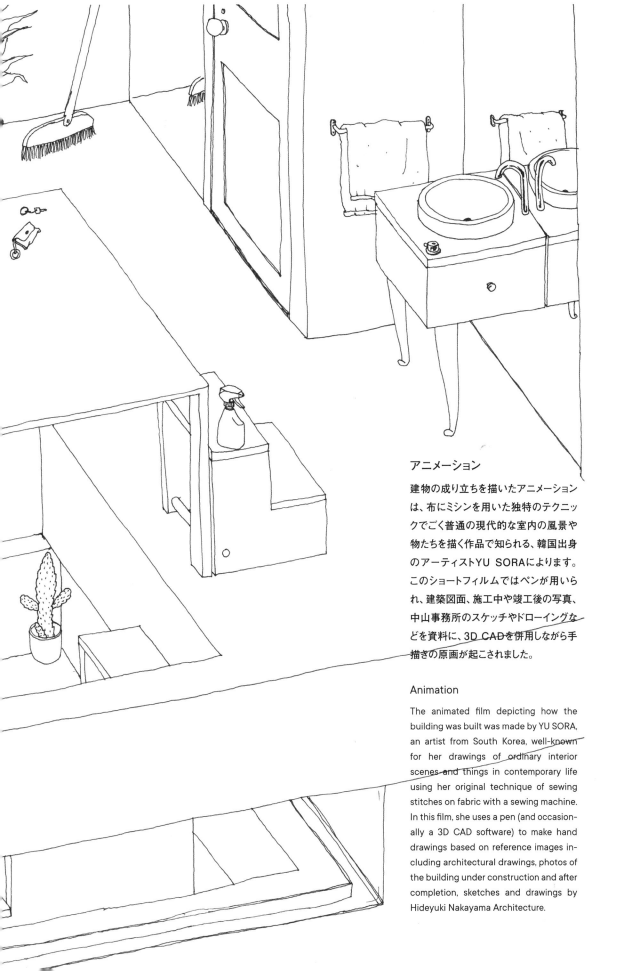

アニメーション

建物の成り立ちを描いたアニメーションは、布にミシンを用いた独特のテクニックでごく普通の現代的な室内の風景や物たちを描く作品で知られる、韓国出身のアーティストYU SORAによります。このショートフィルムではペンが用いられ、建築図面、施工中や竣工後の写真、中山事務所のスケッチやドローイングなどを資料に、3D CADを併用しながら手描きの原画が起こされました。

Animation

The animated film depicting how the building was built was made by YU SORA, an artist from South Korea, well-known for her drawings of ordinary interior scenes and things in contemporary life using her original technique of sewing stitches on fabric with a sewing machine. In this film, she uses a pen (and occasionally a 3D CAD software) to make hand drawings based on reference images including architectural drawings, photos of the building under construction and after completion, sketches and drawings by Hideyuki Nakayama Architecture.

写真

映像に使用されたスチル写真は、写真家 岡本充男によって、竣工後間もない2006年9月、35mmアナログフイルムに撮影されたものです。全430枚の写真は、すべて手持ちのレンジファインダーカメラが用いられました。ファッション写真を主なフィールドとする写真家らしく、人物、物、建築、風景が等価に扱われており、偶然か、建築家による設計当初のスケッチと極めて近い印象となっています。

Photograph

Photographs used in the film were taken by photographer Mitsuo Okamoto using 35mm film, immediately after the completion in September 2006. All of 430 photos were taken using a hand-held range finder camera. Because he is a photographer mainly specializing in fashion, his photos capture people, things, architecture, and scenery with equal intensity, which are coincidentally quite similar to sketches drawn by the architect during the initial design phase.

映像

その後状況が変化して、一時この住宅は空き家となっていました。最後に映るのは、建築家自らがカメラを手に現地を訪れた、2019年3月の映像です。

Film

Later, due to some circumstances, this house was left vacant for a while. The film shown in the last part was shot by the architect himself using a hand-held camera on his visit to the site in March 2019.

Essay

スイスにはチョコレート　中山英之

学生時代、ヒッチコック映画を通してラカンを考える(『ヒッチコックによるラカン』スラヴォイ・ジジェク著)、という刺激的な本に出会ったことをきっかけに、巻末にあった全作品リストにチェックを入れながら、レンタルビデオ店に通い詰めていた時期がありました。背伸びした読書から観はじめたヒッチコックでしたが、すぐに夢中になりました。と同時に「あれ？ この感じは最近の映画で観たことある気がするなあ」とか、また、新しい映画を観ると「ヒッチコックのあれに似てるじゃないか」みたいに思うことがとても多いことに気付きました。当たり前ですよね、アルフレッド・ヒッチコックは言わずと知れたサスペンス映画の神様なのですから。けれどもどうして彼だけが、後の定番となるような映画表現をあんなにも次々と生み出すことができたのでしょうか。

ほどなくして、その秘密に迫った有名なインタビュー集があることを知りました。『映画術』と題されたその本は、当時すでに映画界の新しい波と目されていたあのフランソワ・トリュフォーによって編まれた、つまり同業者による本です。難解なジジェクの本に四苦八苦しながらはじまったヒッチコック映画を観る旅の、僕にとってこの『映画術』は旅行ガイドのような存在でした。

「後の定番」と書きましたが、ということはヒッチコック以前にはまだどこにもなかった技法やアイデアを、そんなもの見たことも聞いたこともないスタッフや役者に理解させることから仕事がはじまるわけです。そうでなくても映画づくりというのは、思い通りにならない天気や風景や他人を手なずける日々でもあるのだから、どこか建築の仕事に似ているな、と勝手に親近感を覚えてしまいます。ヒッチコックはそんな毎日をどんなふうに乗り越えていったのか。本ではその秘密が同じ苦労を知る映画監督の目線から解き明かされていくのですから、おもしろくないわけがありませんよね。

中でも特に記憶に残っているのが「スイスにはチョコレート」というエピソードです。かつては映画館へ出かけることは観客にとって疑似旅行体験だったに違いありません。007シリーズなんて特にそうです。そして、誰もが知っているような観光名所を背景に選ぶことにはもうひとつ、観客にカットのあいだに舞台が別の場所に移動したことを伝える省略の合図としての働きもあるわけです。駅や空港の看板のカットを挟んだり、地図を背景に飛行機の映像を重ねたりするのも、こうした移動表現の定番です。ヒッチコック映画ではどうでしょう。彼はそれをもっと自然にやる方法について考えた。そして、そのための方法のひとつが「スイスにはチョコレート」だったのですね。シーンのなかでさりげなく役者にチョコレートを注文させると、自然とスイスに来た感じが生まれる、というわけです。

「北北西に進路をとれ」(1959、アメリカ)という映画──フランク・ロイド・ライトの住宅をコピーしたセットが出てくるので、建築好きの人にとっても楽しめる映画なのですが──を撮っているときに、ヒッチコックはやっぱり「スイスにはチョコレート」について考えた。この映画はニューヨークからラストのラッシュモア山めがけて北西に移動していく話なので、このベクトルを印象付ける場所として、途中にあるデトロイトに目を付けます。この場合はチョコレートではなく、「デトロイトには自動車工場」となりました。ここから、映画の筋はまだ全然決まってもいないのに、当時最新鋭だった自動車工場の生産ラインを舞台にしたシーンの構想が勝手に出来上がっていきます。

ベルトコンベアの上で、最初はネジ1本だったところからどんどんクルマが組み上がっていきます。ベルトコンベアとその上の流れ作業は、カメラの基本的な動きのひとつである平行移動撮影ととても相性がいいことも、頭にあったのだと思います。その前を、主人公の男と工場長が大事な話をしながら歩いていく。そしてちょうど話し終わった辺りで、背後のライン上でもクルマが1台完成する。その間カメラは長回しのノンストップです。そこで工場長が自慢げに「どうです、すばらしいものでしょう」と言って出来上がったばかりのクルマのドアを開けると、中から死体がごろっと……。何て最高のアイデア！ と思うのですが、ちょっと待てよ、僕の観た「北北西に進路をとれ」にはそんなシーンはありません。本には「このアイデアは最高だったが、違和感なく組み込むプロットが思い付かなくて、やめた」と書いてありました。

具体的なアイデアはもちろんなのですが、最も興味深いのは、映画の全体像が出来ていない段階で、具体的な部分だけが勝手につくられていくことでした。こうした部分的なシーンを考えていく過程で浮上する、カメラの動きまでをも含んだ演出やアイデアというのは、全体像を組み立てていくようなところからはなかなか派生してこない質のものです。そうやって、必ずしも大きな構図から構想されたわけではない部分がどこかで2時間の尺に束ねられたところに、世界がひとつ描かれる。すると私たちは、まるで偶然と偶然が張りめぐらさせた伏線によって、思いもよらない出来事が引き起こされる、その顛末から目が離せなくなってしまう。そのことに、とても興味を惹かれました。

この成り立ち方は、どこか街や都市に似ています。一つひとつの建築や出来事は決して全体から導き出されたわけではない、個々に独立したものだけれど、それらが重なり合い、作用し合ったところに、複雑な、けれども見えないどこかで糸を引き合っているような全体があって、その中をどこまでも歩くことができる。それこそが、私たちにとっての都市の魅力なのだと思います。けれども、どんなにすばらしい中世の街区があっても、それをそっくりコピーすれば素敵な街が出来るのかといえば、そんなことはありません。なのに

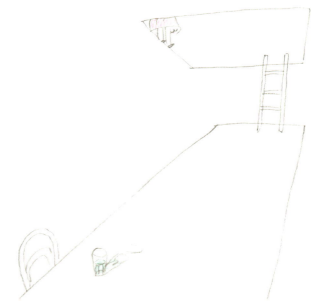

Essay

ヒッチコックの映画を観ると、計画的に組み立てることが本質的にはできない、まるで都市のような感触が、映画というひとつの制作物としてちゃんとデザインされているではありませんか。「スイスにはチョコレート」は僕にとって、その謎に一歩近づく、おまじないのように思われました。

初めて自分の名前で住宅の設計をすることになったとき、僕と仕事を手伝ってくれることになった最初のスタッフにとって、1軒の家とはどこから考えはじめればよいのかまったくわからない存在でした。街にとっては風景の一部だし、家族にとっては生活の場であり、大きいけれど、デザインされた人工物という意味ではコップと変わらないし、そして僕たちにとっては「作品」なる厄介な自意識の対象でもある。その時に思い出したのが、「スイスにはチョコレート」でした。どこから考えはじめればよいのかわからないのなら、いっそそのまま、どこから考えはじめたのかわからないようなものをつくればいいじゃないか、ヒッチコックみたいに！ と、大それたことに僕たちは考えることにしたのです。

僕たちがしたのは、そこにすでにあって、特に意味があるとは思えないものをじっと眺めることで、思い付いたことを片っ端からつくり話にしていくことです。ヒッチコックがベルトコンベアの動きにレール撮影の技法を重ね合わせたように、つくり話にもまだ全体像はないけれど、それがどこかで建築としての必然性と重なり合うように注意しながら、僕たちは自分たちにとってのスイスを見つけては、いったい何がチョコレートなのかを考え続けました。思い付いたらスケッチがまた1枚出来て、それがいくつか溜まったところで、ある日スタッフがそれらをひとつの模型にしてみました。自分たちが考えたつもりのない、けれどもどこかに自分たちのスケッチの一部が見つかるような形がひとつ、出来上がりました。

その住宅は、建物の骨格をつくる工場で、普通は出来上がった家に家具屋さんから最後に届くダイニングテーブルも一緒につくられて、鉄骨屋さんによって工事のはじめに現場に運び込まれました。施主が何気なく「買いたい」と言った素敵な外国製のキャビネットのメーカーに頼み込んで同じ取っ手と色サンプルを取り寄せ、造り付けのキッチンを同じ色に塗って取っ手を取り付けました。現実的に考えれば、物事が決まっていく順番が完全にあべこべだけど、だからといってテーブルがテーブルではないわけではない。

結果として、そこにある物はみんな、どこかでそうであるけれど、どこかではそうでなくもある。そんな状態を僕たちは目指していたのだと思います。誰かが「もしかしたらそうではないのではないか」と思った瞬間に、それまで見えていたつもりのすべての関係が、まったく別の何かに読み替えられてしまうような感覚は、ヒッチコック映画の真骨頂です。映画の神様を前にこんなことを言ってしまっていいのかわからないけれど、僕にとって映画を観ることと建築を考えることは、ずっとそんな仲にあります。

Essay

Chocolate for Switzerland

Hideyuki Nakayama

After reading an inspiring book entitled *Everything You Always Wanted to Know about Lacan (But Were Afraid to Ask Hitchcock)* written by Slavoj Žižek as a student, I made frequent visits to a rental video shop and watched all of Hitchcock's movies, checking off the attached list of his works one by one. While I started watching his movies thanks to this challenging book, I instantly became fascinated with his work. At the same time, I began to notice certain things: for example, I would see one of Hitchcock's movies and say to myself, "Um… I've seen something like this in a recent movie…" or, I would see a new movie and think, "This looks exactly like that movie by Hitchcock." I suppose it is natural, because Alfred Hitchcock is the god of suspense movies. But why was he the only cinema director who was able to create such an endless repertoire of extraordinary cinematic expressions that became "classics" at a later time?

Shortly after that, I discovered a famous interview book entitled *Hitchcock/Truffaut* written by François Truffaut, who was considered a "new wave" cinema director at that time—it was a compilation of interviews with a cinema director by a cinema director. While my journey into the world of Hitchcock's movies had begun with my struggle with the challenging book by Žižek, this book "Hitchcock/Truffaut" became a "travel guide" for me.

The expressions that became "classics at a later time" were still unseen and unheard of before the days of Hitchcock, which meant that Hitchcock's film production started from having his staff and actors comprehend unprecedented techniques and ideas. Film production also involves dealing with unpredictability and uncertainty of the weather, scenery and various people involved, which is somewhat similar to architectural profession—and this is why I feel an affinity with film production. How did Hitchcock manage to survive such hectic days? This book reveals some of his "secret tips" through the eyes of a movie director who knows the challenges in the profession—how could it not be interesting?

One of the most memorable episodes is "Chocolate for Switzerland." Long time ago, going to a cinema must have been equivalent to going on a virtual trip for audiences. For example, the James Bond movie series perfectly served that purpose. Another purpose for showing famous sightseeing spots in the background is to let audiences know that the story moved to a different setting without words. Inserting a brief shot of a train station or airport sign and overlapping images of a map and a flying airplane were among typical expressions of movement. How is movement expressed in Hitchcock's movies? He came up with ways to express it more naturally, and one of such expressions was to use chocolate as a metaphor for Switzerland. Audiences sense a typical "Swiss" atmosphere by watching an actor casually buying a chocolate at a kiosk along the street.

When shooting a movie entitled North by Northwest (1959, USA) — which is a fascinating movie for architecture fans, as it features a Frank Lloyd Wright-inspired house — Hitchcock thought about what would be equivalent to "chocolate for Switzerland" in this case. This movie portrays a northwest-bound journey from New York to Mount Rushmore, and he chooses Detroit among other cities along the way to depict some scenes on the road. In this case, Hitchcock came up with the idea of an "automobile factory for Detroit" instead of chocolate. Although the movie plot wasn't decided at all at this point, he already developed an idea for the automobile factory scene featuring the state-of-the-art production line as follows:

The shot starts from a screw on an assembly line belt conveyor, then various parts are added to the body piece by piece and finally we see a fully assembled car. I suppose Hitchcock was aware that the linear manufacturing sequence on a belt conveyor can be effectively captured using the parallel tracking shot. The main male character and the factory manager are engaged in an important conversation as they walk along the assembly line. Just when they finish the conversation, a car is completed at the same time on the assembly line behind them. The entire scene is shot in one long take, non-stop. Then the factory manager says to the man, "What do you think? Isn't it wonderful?" and opens the door to the car and a corpse falls out... I thought, "What a great idea! But wait a minute... I haven't seen a scene like that in North by Northeast!" and I learned that Hitchcock said, according to the book, "the real problem was that we couldn't integrate the idea into the story."

In addition to his specific idea, I was particularly interested in the fact that the details of particular scenes were developed for its own sake, even though there was not an overall picture of the movie itself. When concentrating on a particular part, it is possible to come up with ingenious ideas, camera movements and more, but it is impossible to achieve the same level of creativity when planning an overall picture. Parts that are not necessarily conceived from the whole are put together into a two-hour long moving image to portray a "world." I was very intrigued with how subplots connecting a series of consequences lead to unexpected events, and how we were not able to keep our eyes off what was happening.

This composition is somewhat similar to how a city or town is planned. While each of the buildings and events there is independent and not necessarily conceived from the whole, they overlap and interact with each other to form a whole, or something like a network of interwoven invisible threads where we can walk around inside forever. I think this experience is what attract us to cities. We cannot make an attractive city by

Essay

simply replicating beautiful medieval city blocks. But in Hitchcock's films, distinct feelings of a city—which inherently cannot be created based on a plan—is perfectly designed in the form of movies. For me, "Chocolate for Switzerland" was like a secret code that helped me unlock Hitchcock's secrets.

When I was given an opportunity to design a house under my name for the first time, my first staff member and I had no idea what to think about first in designing a house. It is part of an urbanscape, a place to live for a family, and a designed artificial object like a glass (although it's much larger), as well as an "architectural work"—or an object of one's troublesome self-consciousness. Then I remembered "Chocolate for Switzerland". We boldly decided that we could make something that people couldn't tell where we started (—like Hitchcock!), if we didn't know where to start.

What we did was by closely observing insignificant existing things that already existed, we wove together random ideas into stories. Just as if Hitchcock associated the parallel tracking shot with the movement of a belt conveyor, we thought about how we could associate our stories with architectural necessities and tried to find out what our "Switzerland" or "chocolate" would be. We sketched out our ideas one after another. When we had a pile of sketches, the junior architect combined all of our ideas into a model. We conceived a form we had never imagined, but nevertheless it contained bits and pieces of ideas drawn in sketches.

Not only the steel frames of the house but also a dining table—which would be normally delivered from a furniture shop after completion—were prefabricated at a steel fabrication factory and delivered to the construction site at the beginning of the construction. When we found that our client was interested in buying a beautiful imported cabinet, we immediately asked the cabinet manufacturer to send us the same type of handles and color sample, painted the kitchen furniture in the same color, and attached the handles. Realistically speaking, we were making decisions in a completely reverse order. But a dining table is a dining table, no matter how we make it.

In the end, things existing there are what they are meant to be, but not what they are meant to be at the same time. I think we wanted to create such conditions. As soon as someone starts to wonder if these things are not what they are meant to be, all relationships between existing things that we took for granted suddenly look totally different—this is exactly a true "Hitchcock" experience.
Maybe I shouldn't say something like this in front of the god of cinema, but the act of seeing a film and the act of thinking about architecture are related in such a way in my mind.

敷地ではなく

この家は、長らく広々とした空き地だった場所があっという間に宅地開発されて、その隅に残された区画に建てられました。クローバーが自生し、そのあいだに小さな虫たちがうごめくただの「地面」だったその場所が、ひとたび宅地化し分譲されると、ブロックで四角く区切られて「敷地」へと名前を変えます。住宅地の隅の「地面」が、この場所だけでも地面のままであるように、建築は上方向に持ち上げて建てられました。

Not a Building Site

This house was built on a remaining vacant land next to residential lots developed from a land that had been left vacant for many years. This place, which had been a plain "ground" naturally covered with clover and full of small moving insects, suddenly turned into "building sites" divided into rectangular blocks as soon as it was developed into residential lots and sold. We raised this build-

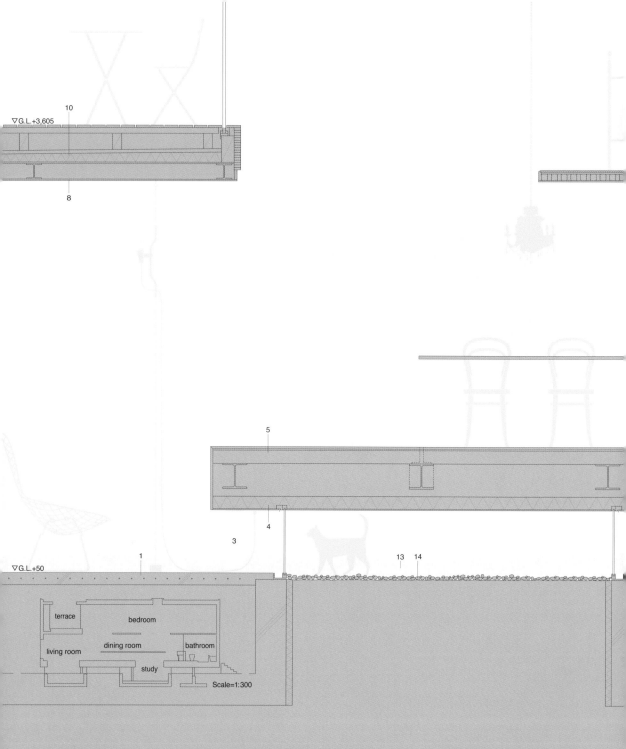

1   dust proofing paint
    100mm concrete around under floor heating
    100mm polystyrene form
2   250mm footing slab
3   150/150mm a lump of steel
    with heat insulasion paint finish
4   6mm silica calcium board
    vapour barrier
    100mm glass wool thermal insulation

5   3mm urethan resin painted floor
    2x12mm structural plywood
    0.2mm floor heating film
    105/45/3.2/455 joists
6   3mm Fiber Reinforced Plastics waterproofing
    2x12mm waterproofed plywood
    100/50/3.2/455 joists(steel)
7   22mm steel plate with Zinc Hot Dip Galvanizings
8   13mm cedar board with AEP
9   8mm saisal carpet
    12mm structural plywood
    50/50/3.2/80 joists(steel)
    3mm Fiber Reinforced Plastics waterproofing

10 white cedar deck
    2x9mm waterproofed plywood
    100mm polystyrene form
11 semitransparent mirror film
    on 10mm tempered glass
12 13mm cedar siding(fire proofed)
    60/30/455 battens (venting layer)
    waterproof membrane
    60mm water-repellent glass wool board 32K
    12mm structural plywood(fire proofed)
13 clover ground cover
14 50mm river gravel

Detailed section   Scale=1:30

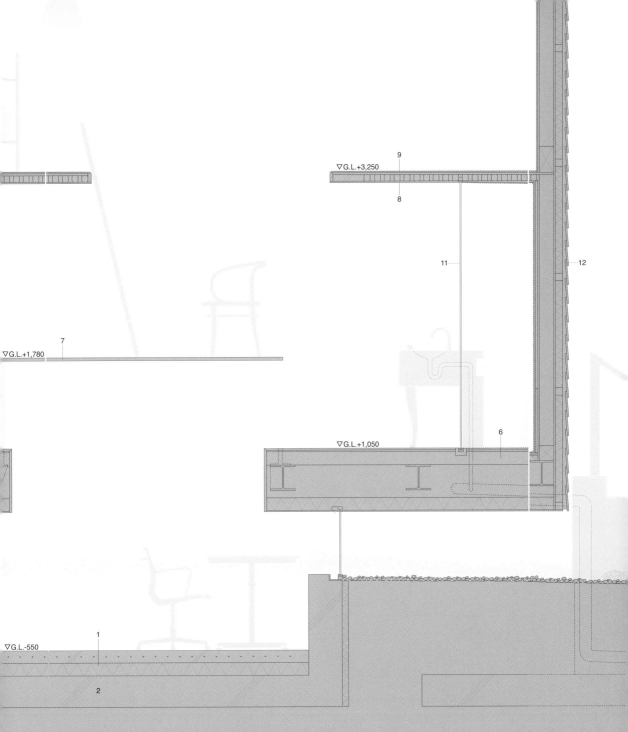

机と床のあいだ

2階建ての大きさに、人が上に立てるほど大きくて頑丈なテーブルを入れると、4つの層が重なっています。デスクチェアに座ると地面に寝転んだ目線になる書斎は、凍結深度まで掘り下げた基礎そのもの。その上の天井も、工事現場でよく使われる「敷鉄板」を転用しただけの簡素なダイニングテーブルですが、テーブルの上に立つと肩まで出てしまうくらい低く薄い2階床には、木口に面取りを施した木材が回され、麻を敷いて家具のように仕立てられています。

Between a Desk and a Floor

A large and sturdy table on which people can stand is placed inside the two-story building composed of four overlapping spatial layers. The study, where one's line of vision aligns with the ground level when sitting on a chair, is located on top of the foundation dug below the frost penetration depth. The ceiling above the study is a tabletop of a dining table made of steel road plates often used at construction sites. The second floor slab is very thin and located very low, just below the level of the shoulder of a person standing on the steel table. The floor is built like furniture with the butt ends finished with wood board with chamfered edges and the surface covered with linen.

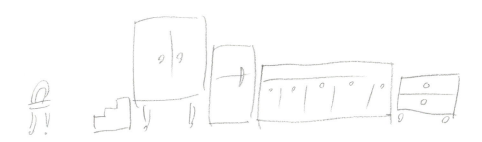

階段ではなく

階段はそこにあるだけでこことどこかを結び付け、そこを行き来する人間の寸法を暗示する存在だけれど、だからといって椅子のように簡単に持ち去れるものではありません。建築は人間のためにつくられるものではあるけれど、世界は人間のためだけにあるわけではないから、建築が時々、大きさのものさしを見失い、空間が時々、人間を忘れるために、階段はアメリカ製の巨大な冷蔵庫の隣で、キャビネットの顔をしています。

Not Stairs

Stairs, just by being there, connect here and somewhere else, while implying the size of people going up and down at the same time. On the other hand, they cannot be carried away so easily like chairs. Architecture is made for people, but the world does not exist only for people. The stairs, located next to the gigantic refrigerator made in USA, pretend to be a cabinet in order to make this architecture lose the sense of scale and make these spaces forget about people sometimes.

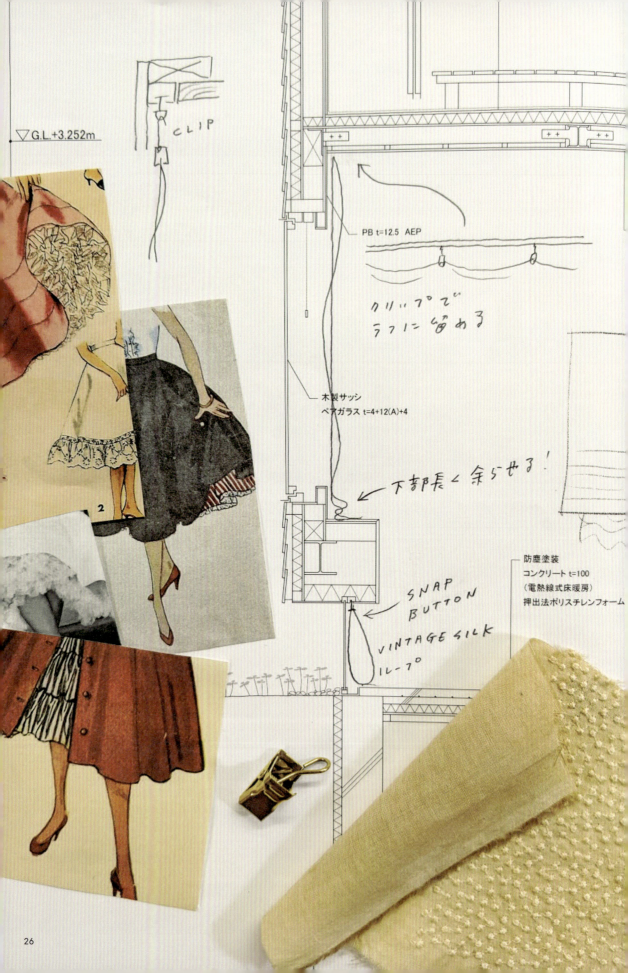

だぶだぶのカーテン

大きすぎる服も、裾を折ったりまくったり、中を体が泳ぐように動いたりすることでその人らしい服になることがあるように、建築に誂えられすぎていないカーテンがあったなら、それはどんなものなのでしょうか。家の下から覗くカーテンは、スカートの下からはみ出してしまったペチコートのように、古いレースの風合いをお手本にした布を、まくり上げるように取り付けてあります。窓よりずっと長いカーテンレールに吊った薄いチュールは、窓の前にぎゅっとまとめると奥が見えなくなります。どちらもテキスタイルデザイナーの安東陽子による仕事です。

Oversized Curtain

Oversized clothes—when worn with the hems turned up or the sleeves rolled up, or when a wearer moves as if he/she is swimming in them—often creatively express one's personal characteristics. Let us imagine curtains that "do not fit the building too perfectly." What kind of curtains would they be? Curtains made of fabric resembling antique lace are shown through the gap under the house. They are turned up and attached to the track, looking like a petticoat showing from under a skirt. Lightweight tulle fabric is hung from a curtain track that is much wider than the window width. When the curtain is gathered in front of the window, it becomes dense and obstructs views from outside. Both of the curtains were created by textile designer Yoko Ando.

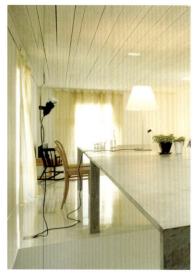

照明のない家

天井のブラケットから吊るされたペンダントライトは、そこがダイニングであることを決めてしまうし、白い壁に仕込まれた間接照明は、そこが寝る場所であることを固定してしまうから、この家の電気図にはいわゆる建築照明がひとつもありません。その代わり多くのコンセントが、隠されたスイッチとネットワークされて、そこにつながれた既成品のライトを、離れた場所から操作することができるように計画されています。

House with No Lights

A suspended lamp hanging from the ceiling bracket indicates the location of a dining room, and indirect lighting embedded in a white wall determines its use as a bedroom. In order to avoid such situations, no built-in lighting is included in the electrical diagram of this house. Instead of built-in lighting, we installed a network of many outlets and concealed switches so that prefabricated lighting fixtures can be connected anywhere and remote-operated.

小さなピロティ

持ち上げられた家の下の小さな「ピロティ」には、屋根とテラスからの樋を通じて雨が降り、キッチンの下引き換気扇から吹く風のあいだを悠々と猫が横切ります。浮いた家につなぐ給排水と給電は、扉の前に置かれた階段の下を通されました。

Very Low Pilotis

The very low "pilotis" under the raised house receives rain coming from roof and terrace drains, lets through trespassing cats as well as the exhaust air from the downward kitchen ventilation fan. Water supply, drainage, and power supply are connected to the raised house through the space under the stairs in front of the door.

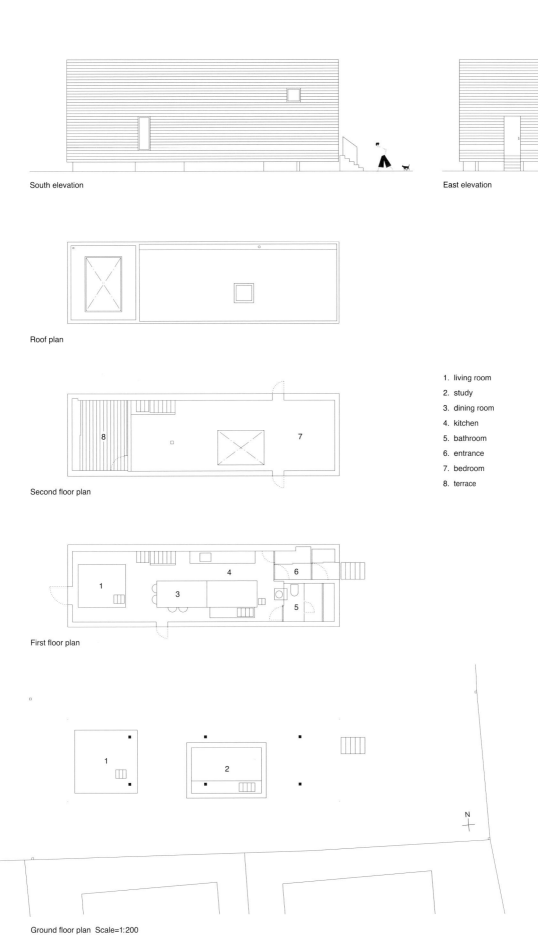

映画「2004」

監督：YU SORA
音楽：庄子 渉

アニメーション：YU SORA
写真：岡本充男
映像：中山英之建築設計事務所
協力：金巻 勲

YU SORA：アーティスト。2011年弘益大学彫塑科（韓国）卒業後、韓国・日本を中心に活動。黄金町バザール2013参加、17年個展「引越し」（YCC gallery）。18年東京ミッドタウンアワード優秀賞。

岡本充男：フォトグラファー。日本大学芸術学部文芸学科卒業。設楽茂男に師事、2004年よりフリーランス。雑誌のほか、広告、書籍、CDジャケットなど幅広い分野で写真を手掛ける。主な受賞歴に、APAアワード2015 広告作品部門優秀賞など。

庄子 渉：音楽家、アートコーディネーター／プロデューサー。東京藝術大学音楽学部卒業。2013年アーティスト・イン・レジデンス「PARADISE AIR」創設、地域資源を活かした創造的な街づくりに取り組む。

書籍

写真・図版
YU SORA：表紙、p. 1、pp. 4-9、pp. 32-33
岡本充男：p.10-11、p. 27（右下・左下）、p. 28（中央下）、p. 29（左下）
矢野紀行：p. 21（上）、p. 24、p. 28（左上・中央上）
新 良太：p. 25（左上・右上）
※上記以外は中山英之建築設計事務所

参考図書
スラヴォイ・ジジェク 著、露崎俊和 訳『ヒッチコックによるラカン――映画的欲望の経済』（トレヴィル、1994）
フランソワ・トリュフォー、アルフレッド・ヒッチコック 著、山田宏一、蓮實重彦 訳『定本 映画術 ヒッチコック／トリュフォー』（晶文社、1991）

建物

所在地：長野県松本市
主要用途：専用住宅

設計：中山英之、名和研二
設計協力：三島香子
構造設計：なわけんジム（名和研二、渡辺 英*）*元所員
施工：アスピア
カーテンデザイン：安東陽子

敷地面積：202.83㎡
建築面積：57.60㎡
延床面積：100.57㎡
階数：地上2階
最高高さ：5,950mm
構造：木造、一部鉄骨造
杭・基礎：ベタ基礎

設計期間：2004年4月-2005年8月
竣工：2006年5月

受賞：SD Review 2004 鹿島賞、第23回吉岡賞
主な掲載誌：『GA HOUSES 93』、『新建築』2006年12月号、『Casa BRUTUS』2007年2月号、『ottagono』2008年2月号

Film *2004*

Director: YU SORA
Music: Wataru Shoji

Animation: YU SORA
Photograph: Mitsuo Okamoto
Film: Hideyuki Nakayama Architecture
Cooperation: Isao Kanemaki

YU SORA: Artist. After graduated from carving and modeling department, Hongik Univ. (Korea) in 2011, Yu has been pursuing creative activities in Korea and Japan. Participated in Koganecho bazaar 2013 and a private exhibition "moving" (YCC gallery) in 2017. Received Tokyo Midtown Award Excellence Prize in 2018.

Mitsuo Okamoto: Photographer. Graduated from Nihon University College of Art and Literary Arts. Sutdied under Shigeo Shitara. Became a freelance photographer in 2004. Okamoto's photos are featured in diverse fields including advertising, books, and CD covers as well as magazines. Received APA award 2015 Excellence Prize among other awards.

Wataru Shoji: Musician, Art coordinator / Producer. Graduated from Tokyo University of the Arts, Faculty of Music. Established the artist in residence "PARADISE AIR" in 2013. Shoji is actively engaged in creative town planning that makes the best use of local resources.

Building

Location: Matsumoto, Nagano, Japan
Main use: Private residence

Architects: Hideyuki Nakayama, Kenji Nawa
Collaborator: Kyoko Mishima
Structural consultants: Nawaken gym (Kenji Nawa, Ei Watanabe*)
*former staff member
General contractor: ASUPIA
Curtain design: Yoko Ando

Site area: 202.83m²
Building area: 57.60m²
Total floor area: 100.57m²
Number of stories: 2 above-floor stories
Maximum height: 5,950 mm
Structure: Wood structure and partly steel frame structure
Pile & foundation: Raft foundation

Design period: April 2004 – August 2005
Completion: May 2006

Awards: SD Review Kajima prize 2004, the 23th Yoshioka prize
Publication: *GA HOUSES 93*, *Shinkenchiku* (December, 2006), *Casa BRUTUS* (February, 2007), *ottagono* (February, 2008)

Book

Images
YU SORA: cover, p. 1, pp. 4–9, pp. 32–33
Mitsuo Okamoto: p. 10–11, p. 27 (right-below, left-below),
p. 28 (center-below), p. 29 (left-below)
Toshiyuki Yano: p. 21 (above), p. 24, p. 28 (left-above, center-above)
Ryota Atarashi: p. 25 (left-above, right-above)
Images not listed above: Hideyuki Nakayama Architecture

Reference
Slavoj Zizek, trans. Toshikazu Tsuyuzaki, *Tout ce que vous avez toujours voulu savoir sur Lacan sans jamais oser le demander à Hitchcock* (Treville, 1994)
François Roland Truffaut Alfred Hitchcock, trans. Koichi Yamada, Shigehiko Hasumi, *Le cinéma selon Alfred Hitchcock (revised edition)*, (Shobunsha, 1991)

mitosaya botanical distillery

mitosaya薬草園蒸留所

(2018年竣工)

mitosaya botanical distillery

(Completed in 2018)

カメラ　江口宏志　企画　川村真司

人が来なくなってしまい、静かに閉園した薬草園と展示室を、果物とハーブを使った蒸留所に生まれ変わらせる計画。とはいえ、広大な敷地や既存の建物はほとんどがほったらかしの手付かずです。その場所にあるものをそのままに、けれども自分たちなりの方法で少しずつ読み替えていくことで、そこにない何かを生み出していく。動きはじめたばかりのお酒づくりの日々を、一人称カメラが見つめます。

Camera: Hiroshi Eguchi　Planning: Masashi Kawamura

An abandoned former medicinal plant botanical garden is renovated into a distillery producing spirits using fruits and herbs. We create something that does not exist there by looking at existing things on the site as they are and gradually reinterpreting them in our own ways. A camera observes the just-opened distillery's production processes from a first-person point of view.

Film

http://hideyukinakayama.com/cinema/02

蒸留所の5つのドア
江口宏志

広大な畑の向こうに朝日が昇ってくる。徐々に明るくなった窓から、ついばみながら歩き回っている鶏たちが見える。朝ごはんを食べ終わり、いつものつなぎと帽子を身に着け、長靴を履き、目の前の蒸留所に向かう。掃き掃除をしていると同僚のオッティがやってきて、簡単なあいさつをして今日やることを話す。

「そろそろサッカー場の梨がいい感じだから収穫しにいこうか。収穫物を入れるかごと棒をバンに積み込んでクリストフが母屋の方から眠そうな顔で出てくる。
「ハイ、ヒロシ。元気？ 今週も忙しいよ」
続いて出てきた妻のクリスティーヌが言う。
「ヤギに赤ちゃんが生まれたんだけど、1匹ミルクを飲まない子がいるの。悪いんだけどしばらくユウコにミルクをあげる係をやってもらえない？ 私が赤いダウンを着ていたから、ミルクをあげる人は赤って覚えてしまったみたい。ダウンを玄関先に置いておくわ」

といって家庭のようにただ日々の生活があるわけではない。そういえば、夕方になるとおいさつもないくいつの間にかみんながいなくなってしまうのも最初はけっこう驚きだった。誰に言われるわけでもなく各々が役割を果たしていて、植物や動物の都合でやることは日々違う。それらを束ねてひとつの物語のようなものが進んでいく。

僕がドイツで学んだのは蒸留酒のつくり方ではあるけれど、同時に教わったのは仕事や生活をないまぜにしつつ円滑に進めていく、ということかもしれない。

だから、中山さんと日本で蒸留所をつくると決めたときに、場所の条件として挙げたのは、日々の生活と、果樹や植物を育てる畑、それらを加工してつくる蒸留酒の製造、その3つが同じ敷地内で分かれることなく混じり合っているということだった。

しかし言うは易しで、そのような場所は実はなかなかない。住居は住居、畑は畑、工場は工場。土地は用途に応じて明確に区分されていて、それをまたいだ場所をつくるには、たとえば山林など用途の決まっていない場所を拓いて、自分でイチからつくる必要がある。それにはもちろんお金も時間も途方もなく掛かってしまう。

だから、元薬草園を利用する事業者を募集する町のサイトを見つけたときは心が躍った。500種類を超える薬草が植生する広大な土地があり、蒸留所やショップ、住居に転用できるいくつかの建物があり、何しろ用途が自由であるということ。あ

Introduction

まりに興奮したので、検索順位が上がらないように(?)募集ページをしばらく見ないようにしたほどだ。

「mitosaya薬草園蒸留所」は、文字通り薬草園でもあり蒸留所でもある。そして僕らが暮らす場所でもある。日々成長する植物たちの手入れや収穫を行い、生産者から仕入れた果物とともに醸造・発酵させ、蒸留する。妻は絵を描き、子どもたちは学校に通う。そしていつの間にか住み着いた2匹の猫も大事な仲間だ。昼間は気ままに遊び、ごはん時にはしっかりと家に帰ってくる。夜は僕の脱ぎっぱなしのコートの上で丸まって2匹で眠っている。

改修に取り掛かる前に何度も話したのは、この場所をどのようにしていきたいかということだった。

少量多品種、高品質な蒸留酒をつくるための、効率的・機能的な製造工場であること。多種多様な薬草を栽培する場所として、開かれた場所にしたいということ。家族や働く人たちが快適に毎日を過ごせるようにすること。などたくさんのことを挙げた。

中山さんに一度ドイツを訪れてもらって、いくつかの蒸留所を一緒に回ったときの体験も役に立った。だいていは家族で運営する小さな蒸留所で、広大な果樹園や酪農そして蒸留所を行うための工夫がなされていた。食後に瓶を並べていろいろな蒸留酒をちょこっとずつ楽しむという

生活の喜びを共有できたのもよかった気がする。

改修については、建築家に任せてもらう方が正確だろうから、この後のページに任せるけれど、日々この場所で過ごす者として、足を踏み入れた人が必ず歓声を上げる、楕円形のホールにある5つのドアのことを書かないわけにはいかない。工程によって明確に区分けされた5つの空間は、作業の切り替えや、衛生状態の保持にとても有効だ。しかし同時にかなりやっかいな存在でもある。1日に何度も行き来するこの両開きのドアを開けるとき、たいていはカードを引いていたり、何かを両手に持っていたりしている。そのためドアを使ってドアノブを引き下げ、つま先でドアを引っ張り出すことになる。道具を忘れたり、やり残したことがあれば、その分行き来は多くなる。自然と行き来を少なくするようモノの配置を見直し、作業効率を考える。

ドイツの蒸留所では僕は脇役、いやエキストラか観客かという立場だったが今は違う。要の登場人物のひとりであり、監督のような立場でもある。ここに関わる人たちが、それぞれの役割をスムーズに果たして、ひとつの物語をつくっていくと。窓の形が違う5つのドアはそんなことをいつも僕に考えさせる。

Five Doors in the Distillery
Hiroshi Eguchi

The morning sun rises over the vast fields. I can see chickens walking around and pecking at the ground through the window as the sun gradually becomes brighter outside. After breakfast, I put on my usual overall, hat, and boots, and head to the distillery in front of our house. While I sweep the floor, one of my colleagues, Otti walks in and we exchange brief greetings and discuss our plans for the day:

"Let's go pick pears by the football field—they are getting ripe. Will you load the harvest baskets and sticks into the van?"

"Hi, Hiroshi. How are you? We have another busy week ahead."

Then, his wife Christine says,

"Our goat had babies, but one of them won't take bottle. Would you ask Yuko to bottle feed it for a while? The baby goat seems to think that a person wearing red gives milk, because I was wearing a red down jacket when I fed it. She can use my down jacket that's hung at the entrance."

When I, along with my wife Yuko, was working as a live-in apprentice at the distillery in Germany, we used to have conversations like this all the time. They had no clear rules or rigid hierarchical relationships like those in companies. By the way, I was quite surprised in the beginning that everyone just leaves from work without saying anything at the end of the workday. Everyone fulfills their respective roles without being told what to do and weaves a story together every day. In addition to learning how to make distilled spirits, I also learned how to combine work and life and lead my life smoothly in Germany.

When I decided to collaborate with Hideyuki to build my distillery in Japan, I told him that I wanted to find a place where three things, namely daily life, fields to grow fruits and plants and production of distilled spirits using crops from the fields blend naturally on the same site.

But that's easier said than done because it is difficult to find a place like that. A residential site for a house. A field for a vegetable field. An industrial site for a factory. Land is clearly categorized into different uses and if you want to combine different uses on a site, you would have to buy a property without a designated use (such as a land in the mountain or forest) and develop the land from its natural state. It would certainly cost a lot of money and time.

When I found a website of a town holding a competition for the selection of a legal entity willing to undertake the reuse of a former medicobotanical garden, my heart leapt with joy. It is a vast land where five hundred species of herbal plants naturally grow. There are several buildings that can be converted into a distillery, a shop, and a house and most of all, there is no restriction on land use. I became very excited and tried not to see access the competition webpage for a while so that the website's search engine ranking wouldn't increase.

Mitosaya botanical distillery is literally a botanical garden and a distillery. It is also our home.

Introduction

We take care of plants that keep growing every day, harvest them, mix them with fruits directly purchased from producers, brew, ferment, and distill the mixture to make brandy. My wife draws and paints, and our kids go to school. Two stray cats, which settled down here before we knew it, are now an important part of our family. They go out to play during the day, come home at dinner time, and sleep on my coat I left lying around at night.

Before starting renovation, I had discussions with Hideyuki numerous times regarding what type of place I wanted.
I told him many things I wanted, including an efficient and functional production facility to make high-quality distilled spirits in small quantities with wide varieties, an open botanical garden to grow a wide variety of medicinal plants, an environment where my family and employees can live and work here comfortably every day and more.
Hideyuki visited me in Germany and we traveled together to see several distilleries. This experience was very helpful. Most of the distilleries we visited were small family-owned distilleries each of which was ingeniously organized to achieve efficient operation of vast orchids, dairy farming, and a distillery with a small number of people.

In addition, I am glad that we were able to share "the joy of life" with the people at the distilleries, an after-dinner moments when we lined up different kinds of distilled spirits on the table and tasted a little bit of each.

As for the renovation, I leave it to Hideyuki to explain in the following pages, as I think the architect can describe the details more accurately. But as a person who lives in this place every day, I have to write about the five doors in an elliptical hall, where people exclaim with delight as soon as they step inside.
Five spaces that are clearly divided according to conditions in the respective processes facilitate the smooth transfer between different works and help maintain hygiene effectively. But they are rather inconvenient at the same time. When we open these double doors many times a day, we are usually pushing hand carts or have our hands full, which means that we need to push and pull down the door knob using an elbow and pull on the door using a toe. When we forget some tool or something to do, we have to go back and forth more frequently. In order to reduce the time of going back and forth, we need to revise the layout of things and improve work efficiency.

I was a supporting actor—or perhaps an extra or a spectator—at the distillery in Germany. But now, I am one of the main actors and also a director. How do we, those involved in this place, weave a story together while playing our respective roles smoothly? The five doors, each with their different-shaped window, always make me contemplate about this question.

Design Notes

蒸留所ができるまで
Story of the Distillery

中山英之
Hideyuki Nakayama

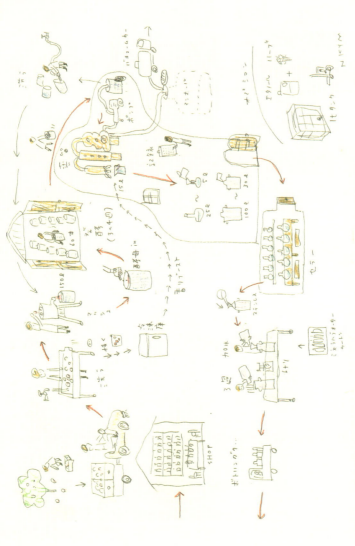

2016年5月、ドイツ、スティーレ・ミューレ蒸留所に修行中の江口一家を訪ねたとき、僕は蒸留と醸造の違いもよくわかっていませんでした。江口さんに各施設やさまざまな設備を案内してもらいながら、果実がブランデーになるまでの工程を忘れぬように書き留めることからはじめました。

When I visited Hiroshi Eguchi, then an apprentice distiller, and his family at the Stählemühle Distillery in Germany in May 2016, I didn't even know the difference between distillation and brewing. Hiroshi showed me around the respective distilling facilities and equipment, and I took a note of the entire distilling process of turning fruits into brandy so as not to forget it.

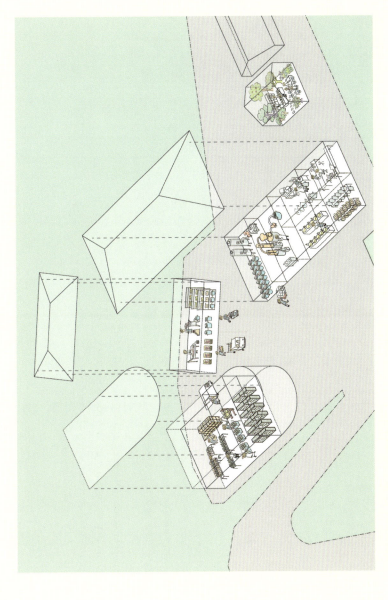

蒸留所候補地が決まるまで、江口さんは帰国のたび全国にいろいろな場所を訪ね歩きました。そんななか出会ったのが、日本がバブルに浮かれていた時代に開園し、その後閉鎖されてしまった薬草園でした。生薬の展示室や研修のための建物など、既存の建築に大雑把に機能を割り振ってみると、すべてがぴったり収まりそうです。みな「ここになら、うまくいくかもしれない」と感じました。

On each trip back to Japan, Hiroshi had visited many places across the country until he decided on a site for his distillery. Eventually, he came across a medicinal botanical garden which had opened during the bubble economy period in Japan and closed down after a while. We roughly allocated necessary functions to various buildings in the existing facility including a herbal plant display room and a training building, and everything seemed to fit into place. We all felt that we could make it happen here.

Design Notes

そんなふうに決まった運命の場所でしたが、初めて訪ねたとき、その場所がいい意味でもそうでない意味でも「立派であることとし少しだけ戸惑いました。特に大きな鉄の門扉から続くアスファルト舗装の坂道は、これからスタートする小さな蒸留所には不釣り合いに思えて、しばし考え込んでしまいました。

ある時、鉄の門扉の脇にひっそりと、かつてその場所にあった受水槽の点検用に付けられた小さな階段を見つけました。試しにその階段から敷地内に入ってみると、木々のあいだを抜けて薬草園を横切り、それまで裏手だと思い込んでいた側から蒸留所へと至る、絵本のページをめくるような道順が浮かび上がってきました。

So, when I first visited this place where he was destined to discover after a long search, I was a bit overwhelmed by its somewhat "stately" atmosphere. The large metal garden gates and the asphalt-paved ramp seemed especially out of proportion with the scale of the small distillery he was going to start.

One day, I spotted small stairs originally built for water tank inspection next to the steel garden gates. I tried entering the site via the stairs—and surprisingly I found a beautiful path among the trees that leads across the medicinal botanical garden and reaching the distillery from (what we had assumed to be) the backside of the building. The entire sequence along the path unfolds as if turning the pages of a picture book.

約270m²の平屋の「管理棟」は、蒸留所に必要な最低限の設備がちょうどよく収まる広さでした。既存の壁をなるべく解体せずに済むこと。作業ごとに異なる環境の部屋を順序よく行き来できること。その様子を訪ねたゲストが眺めることができること。それらを最も単純な方法で実現するプランを考えました。

アメリカ式のお酒をつくる工場は大きなワンルームに工程順に装置を並べていくのに対して、ドイツ式では工程毎に最適な大きさと温湿度の部屋を用意するのだそうです。この蒸留所はもちろんドイツ式。扉をたくさん付けなければならないけれど、それが仕事にとっても、ゲストにとっても、すっきりと、そして楽しい場所であるために、角のない壁にぐるっと並べてみることを思い付きました。それぞれの扉に付けられた窓からは、輸入された蒸留器やものの使われることがなく、20年以上倉庫に眠っていたドイツ製の蒸留器や、小豆島のお醤油屋さんから譲り受けた発酵樽など、この計画を応援してくださる方々に託された大切な道具たちを見ることができます。

The one-story administration building with the floor area of approximately 270m² was just the right size to accommodate minimum necessary equipment for distillation. The existing walls should be preserved as much as possible. Distillers should be able to freely move between different work rooms with respective environmental conditions. The spaces should be arranged in such a way that guests can watch the work process. We carefully worked out floor plans so that these conditions are realized in the simplest way possible.

We learned that the German style liquor factory consists of different rooms designed for respective work processes with the optimum room size, temperature and humidity, while the American style liquor factory, on the contrary, consists of a large open-plan room where different types of equipment for respective work processes are placed in rows. This distillery is naturally based on the German style, which means that we need to install many doors. We thought that these doors should be placed neatly in an enjoyable space, and conceived an idea of installing doors along a curved wall enclosing a space without corners. A window opened in each door allows people to look inside each room where they find precious tools given by supporters of this project, including a German still which had been kept in a storage for twenty years and a fermentation barrel given by a soy sauce manufacturer in Shodoshima.

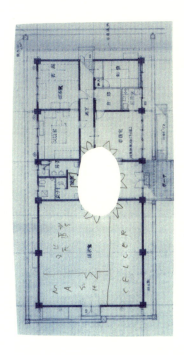

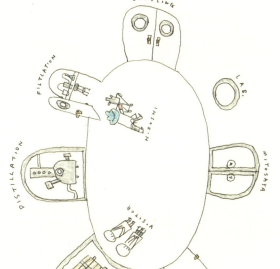

Rooms

発酵室

生薬の展示室を転用した発酵室は、安全な空気環境のために天井を抜いて気積を増やし、排水のために床を上げる以外はほとんど手を加えていません。

Fermentation Room

As for the fermentation room, we removed the entire ceiling to provide sufficient air volume. Because considerable amount of water is used in this room, the floor is raised to accommodate a drain system underneath. The rest of the room is left as it is.

蒸留室

蒸留器とは、発酵させた原料を沸かし、特定の温度で沸点に達したアルコール分だけを逃さないように捕まえる装置です。装置からの熱気を逃がさないと蒸留室がサウナのようになってしまうので、天井の形を工夫します。既存の排煙窓を熱気抜きに見立てて、そこからの光をホールの採光と兼ねる計画です。

Distillation Room

A still is an apparatus used to boil fermented fruit juice and extract alcoholic content when it reaches a boiling point at a specific temperature. The ceiling of the distillation room is carefully shaped to facilitate heat exhaust and prevent the room from turning into a sauna. The existing smoke exhaust windows are used to exhaust heat and let natural light into the hall.

Rooms

セラー

セラーは蒸留したお酒を寝かせる場所。温度管理が大切です。よって、窓のない部屋にはぐるっと断熱材が吹き付けられます。普通は仕上げに覆われてしまう材料ですが、もこもことした質感がカーヴ（洞窟）のようなので、隠さずそのままにしてしまうことにしました。

Cellar

The cellar is a place to age distilled liquor, which requires careful temperature control. Therefore, this room has no windows and is entirely covered with spray-on thermal insulation material. While thermal insulation is usually covered with some finish material, we decided to leave it exposed because we liked its cave-like materiality.

ラボ・ボトリング室

蒸留したてのブランデーは高濃度なため、一部は濾過してから加水し、ラベルに記載されるアルコール濃度に仕上げます。ボトリングまでを行うこの部屋は清潔第一。照明を含むあらゆる機器は、透明な天井の上に密閉されます。南の窓辺には新しいレシピを研究するためのデスクが置かれて、ホールから小窓を覗くと、その様子を見ることができます。

Laboratory / Bottling Room

Freshly distilled brandy, which contains a high level of alcohol, is filtered and watered down to the alcohol percentage indicated on the bottle label. This room, also used for bottling, requires a high level of cleanliness. All types of equipment including lighting fixtures are installed in a sealed space above the transparent ceiling. A desk used for recipe development is placed by the south window, and one can see Hiroshi working on a new recipe at the desk through a small window.

Hall

Section sketch

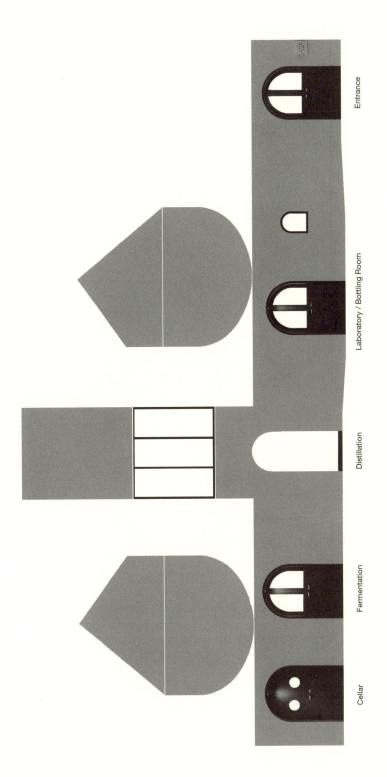

Cellar Fermentation Distillation Laboratory / Bottling Room Entrance

Scale=1:100

Development

Doors

洒落たアーチ形のドアは、正面に残した既存の開口に做った形です。ただしカートを引いて毎日何度も開閉されるドアですから、頑丈な自閉装置や順位調整器が取り付けられた工場仕様です。アーチ形は見学者の側に、それらの機器を見せないための形でもあります。

The elegant arched doors are modeled after existing openings in the front facade. Considering the fact that they are constantly opened and closed, and hit by hand carts every day, they are designed like factory doors with robust self-closing devices and door closure regulators. Another purpose for using arched shapes is to conceal the devices from visitors' views.

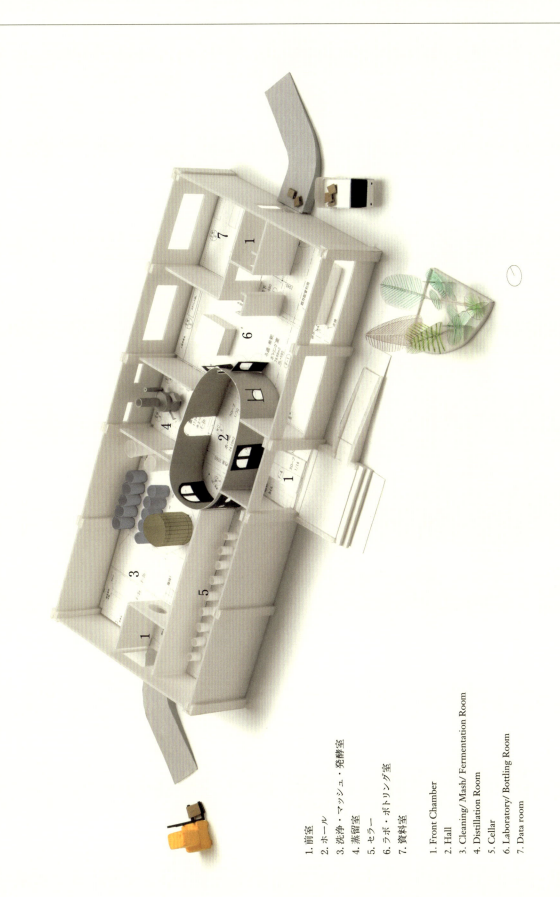

1. 前室
2. ホール
3. 洗浄・マッシュ・発酵室
4. 蒸留室
5. セラー
6. ラボ・ボトリング室
7. 資料室

1. Front Chamber
2. Hall
3. Cleaning/ Mash/ Fermentation Room
4. Distillation Room
5. Cellar
6. Laboratory/ Bottling Room
7. Data room

Map

新しく発見した動線の最後の階段を上ってみると、はじめは裏通りのように感じられていた道が小さなブールバードのように考えていた。それまでは建物の側面でしかなかった場所に、TAKAIYAMA inc. がデザインした蒸留棟のサインを入れることにしました。稼働をはじめた蒸留所のほかにも、家族の住み処や製品を並べるショップなど、まだまだ仕事は山積みです。

When I climbed up the last step of the newly-found stairs, the path which we had formerly regarded as a "back street" began to look like a small boulevard. We decided to place a new sign for the distillery designed by TAKAIYAMA inc. on the wall which we had formerly regarded as a "side wall." We still have so much work to do including a house for the family and a store to sell their products, in addition to the remaining work in the distillery that already started operation.

Credits

Film *mitosaya botanical distillery*

Camera: Hiroshi Eguchi Planning: Masashi Kawamura

Hiroshi Eguchi: Distiller. Established the bookstore UTRECHT in 2002 and started the annual book event currently called "Tokyo Art Book Fair" in 2009. In 2015, he resigned from both and relocated to Germany to learn the making process of distilled spirits in Stählemühle in Germany. In 2017, he renovated the former medicobotanical garden in Otaki, Chiba Prefecture and established Mitosaya Botanical Distillery.

Masashi Kawamura: Creative director. Founded "PARTY" and "dot by dot" and merged the two companies to establish "Whatever" as the company's CCO in 2018. Selected among the Creative magazine's "50 Creators in the World" and the Fast Company Magazine's "100 Most Creative People in Business."

Book

Images
Hideaki Hamada: cover, p. 35
Hiroshi Eguchi: pp. 38–41, p. 42 (left-below, center-below), p. 52 (left)
Go Itami: p. 46 (left-below), p. 47 (below), p. 48 (left), p. 49 (above, right-below)
ONESTORY: p. 46 (left-below, right), p. 47 (above), p. 48 (right), p. 49 (left-below), p. 52 (right)
Images not listed above: Hideyuki Nakayama Architecture

Building

Location: Chiba Main use: Distillery

Architects (renovation): Hideyuki Nakayama Architecture (Hideyuki Nakayama, Kyoko Mishima, Oshi Matsumoto, Yoshifumi Hashimoto*, Takuro Kato) * former staff members
Structural consultants: Ohno Japan (Hirofumi Ohno) General contractor: Sawa Construction
Distiller installation: Tatsumi Seisakusyo Sign: TAKAIYAMA inc.
Lighting equipment: Mintage (Cellar), Toki corporation (Hall doors), Iwasaki Electric (Fermentation room)

Site area: 15,741.52m² Building area: 286.98m² Total floor area: 268.68m²
Number of stories: 1 above-ground floor Maximum height: 8,000mm
Structure: RC frame structure, with steel roof structure
Pile & foundation: Independent footing foundation

Design period: June 2016 – December 2017 Completion: April 2018

54-55

映画「mitosaya 薬草園蒸留所」

カメラ：江口宏志 企画：川村真司

江口宏志：蒸留家。書店「ユトレヒト」、「TOKYO ART BOOK FAIR」立ち上げを経て、2015年、ドイツで蒸留酒造りを学ぶ。17年、千葉県・大多喜町にて「mitosaya 薬草園蒸留所」設立。

川村真司：クリエイティブディレクター。「PARTY」、「dot by dot」設立、2018年「Whatever」として合併、同社CCO。『Creativity』誌「世界のクリエイター50人」、『Fast Company』誌「ビジネス界で最もクリエイティブな100人」に選出。

書籍

写真・図版
濱田英明：表紙、p. 35
江口宏志：pp. 38-41, p. 42（左下・中央下）, p. 52（左）
伊丹豪：p. 46（左上）, p. 47（下）, p. 48（左）, p. 49（上, 右下）
ONESTORY：p. 46（左下・右）, p. 47（右下）, p. 48（上）, p. 49（左下）, p. 52（右）
※ 上記以外は中山英之建築設計事務所

建物

所在地：千葉県 主要用途：蒸留所

設計（既存改修）：中山英之建築設計事務所（中山英之、三島香子、松本巨志、橋本吉史*、加藤拓郎）* 元所員
構造設計：オーノJAPAN（大野博史） 施工：沢工務店 蒸留器接続：タツミ製作所
サイン：TAKAIYAMA inc.
照明器具：ミンテイジ（セラー）、トキ コーポレーション（ホールドア）、岩崎電気（発酵室）

敷地面積：15,741.52 ㎡ 建築面積：286.98 ㎡ 延床面積：268.68 ㎡
階数：地上1階 最高高さ：8,000mm
構造：RCラーメン構造（小屋組みは鉄骨造） 杭・基礎：独立

設計期間：2016年6月-2017年12月 竣工：2018年4月

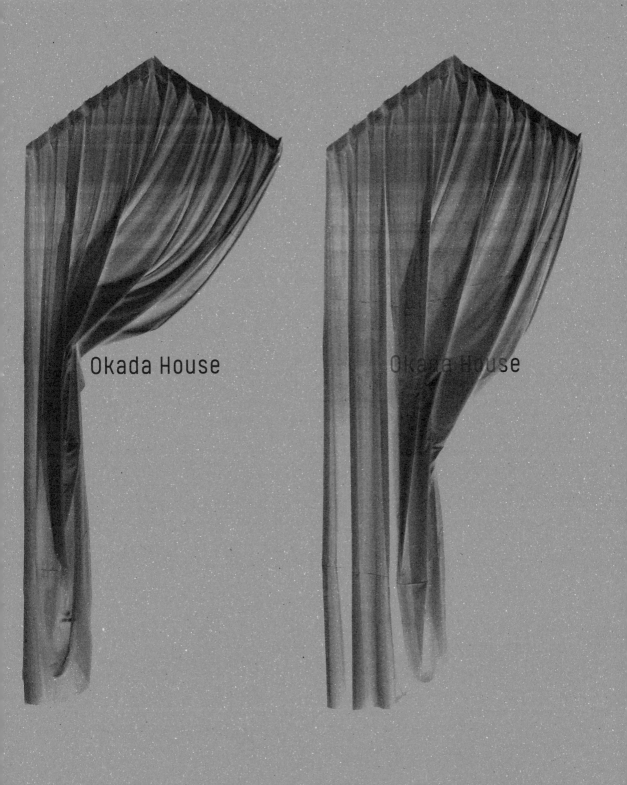

岡田邸
(2009年竣工)

Okada House
(Completed in 2009)

監督　岡田栄造　空間現代
音楽　空間現代

街かどに吊るされた高さ7mのカーテン。その奥に続く、どこかで見たホテルの廊下のような空間。そこかしこに散らばる生活の断片が、静止画のように切り取られます。この映像のために新たに録音された空間現代の音楽は、住み手自らによる撮影と編集に深く関係付けられながら、度重なる対話を経て制作されました。

Director: Eizo Okada / Kukangendai
Music: Kukangendai

7m long curtains are hanging at a street corner. Behind the curtains, there is a familiar looking hotel corridor-like space. Fragments of daily life in the house are framed like still images. Kukangendai's new recording for this film was made through many discussions while closely relating it with film shooting and editing by the director himself who lives in the house.

FILM

http://hideyukinakayama.com/cinema/03

制作会議

岡田栄造 × 空間現代

第1回制作会議
2018年10月24日　「O邸*」にて

この家の住み手でもある岡田栄造の案内で「O邸」を見学後、試作映像を観ながら会議がはじまった。
＊「岡田邸」の建築名称

岡田栄造：さて、どうしましょうか？

空間現代／古谷野慶輔：映像カットのテンポに音を合わせてもいい気がします。フレーズが変わる部分や、変わらない部分があったり。たまに画面がスプリットしていてもいいのかな。

空間現代／野口順哉：たとえば「O邸」の下屋の部分は「外だった部分に増築した中（なか）」という設定になっていますよね。「元外設定の中」みたいな場所。逆に庭は「元中設定の外」だったりする。この建築は中と外というふたつの意味が錯綜しているわけですが、音楽もふたつのフレーズをつくって、例えばスプリットのときはそれぞれに鳴っているという感じです。

古谷野：撮影で録音されている音も使いたい。録音されたシーンではないところで、その音が鳴るというのもありだと思います。

Production Meeting

Eizo Okada × Kukangendai

First Meeting at *O house**,
October 24, 2018

After a tour of the *O House* guided by director Eizo Okada who is also one of the residents of the house, they started a production meeting for the film while watching a rough cut.
＊Architectural title of *Okada House*

Okada: So, what do you think?

Kukangendai/Koyano: We can probably edit music in sync with the cutting rhythms. Maybe we can switch to a new phrase in some parts or continue the same phrase in other parts. We can also split the screen once in a while.

Kukangendai/Noguchi: Two meanings, namely the "interior" and "exterior" are intertwined in this architecture—for example, the attached annex is an "interior space that was originally exterior." Conversely, the garden is "an exterior space that was originally interior." Why don't we make two musical phrases for respective meanings? For example, when the screen splits, we can play the two phrases simultaneously.

Koyano: I want to use sounds recorded during the filming. We could even use some sounds for a scene not related to the original scene where they were recorded.

Noguchi: We can place speakers and film them playing our music.

Okada: I like your idea. The outcome would be quite different from

PRODUCTION MEETING

野口：スピーカーを置いて、われわれがつくった音が鳴っているところを撮るというのもあるかな。

岡田：いいですね。映像の後に音楽を付けたのとは違うものになります。

野口：あとこの建物って、中か外か？って考え出すと「あれ？どっちだっけ？」って気がしてきますが（笑）。音楽と映像の関係も、室内のスピーカーから流れてくる音なのか、後で編集で入れた音なのか、「どっちなんだろう？」って一瞬思わせる仕掛けがあるといいと思う。
岡田さんからわれわれに何か希望みたいなものはありますか？

岡田：うーん……。この家は結構おしゃれなものに見られるんですけど、実はそんなことは全然なくて。変な家なんですよね（笑）。住んでいるわれわれも全然おしゃれではなくて、散らかっているし、むりやり住んでいる。
それとは別に結構怖い家でもあって。いろいろな関係が入れ子になったり、関係が相対的に入れ替わったり、外と中の関係が延々と変わり続けるみたいな感じがある。
だから、「おしゃれじゃない！」という感じにしてほしい（笑）。この家は、そんな生易しいものではないぞ、と。空間現代のみなさんとつくることで、そこが伝わるものにしたい。

一同：（笑）。

岡田：空間現代の音楽が今回の映像に乗っかったら、この家のこれまでの見方が変わる、ということを期待しています。あと、今回はミュージックビデオにならないことがすごく大事だと思っているんです。あくまで「映像の音楽」であること。

野口：音楽に関していえば、映像と関係なくふたつのフレーズをつくって、映像を音楽にむりくり合わせることもできるし。ひとつのフレーズだけを使って、家の中でスピーカーから鳴ってるものと、編集で後乗せしたものとでふたつとすることもできます。

a film with music added later after filming.

Noguchi: When you start wondering if this building is inside or outside, you'd think "so which is it?" (Laughs.) It would be interesting to have one wonder for a moment if the music is coming out of the speakers in the film or if it was added later when editing the film and make one think, "Well... which is it?"
Do you have any requests for us?

Okada: Umm... People seem to think this house is rather stylish, but actually, it is not stylish at all. It's a strange house... (laughs.) We are not stylish and our house is messy, but we just manage to live there.
The other thing is, it is also pretty scary. Some space is nested within another space while other spaces are interchanged. And the relationship between inside and outside keeps changing forever. So, I want your music to express... something like "our house is not stylish!" (laughs)... or "it's not as easy as you might think!" I want to work with you all because I believe Kukangendai's music can communicate this message.

All: (Laughs.)

Okada: I expect that people's perception of this house will change when Kukangendai's music is added to the film. In addition, I think it is crucial that we stay away from making something like a music video. It should simply be music for a film.

Noguchi: In terms of music, we can make two phrases unrelated to the film and somehow edit the film in sync with the music. Or, we can use just one phrase to make two kinds of sounds—one coming out of a speaker inside the house and the other added to the film later.
It would be interesting to place a speaker playing music on the second floor and film it from immediately below and inside of the house, and also from the attached annex across the wall. The speaker can also be placed not just on the second floor, but here or outside.

Kukangendai/Yamada: I suppose the idea is to change the sense of distance of sounds in each cut.

スピーカーを2階に置いて音を鳴らしておいて、すぐ真下の母屋から撮る映像と、壁を隔てた下屋から撮る映像とがある、というのもおもしろいかもしれません。2階だけでなく、こちらの部屋とか、外に置くとかでもいいですね。

空間現代／山田英晶：カットによって音の距離感が変わるということね。

野口：そう。ドアの開閉でも聞こえ方が違ってくる。でもその関係が定着してきたら、それを逆手に取ってスピーカーの位置を変えて撮る。そうすると空間がわからなくなる。

古谷野：同じフレーズが、最初は映像内の音とは別に、「編集で乗せた音」として聞こえているけれど、どこかのポイントで「家の中で鳴っている」感じになるとか。
フレーズに合わせて編集されているところと、映像に合わせて音がぶつ切りになっちゃうところ、どちらもあっていいかもしれない。

野口：スピーカーからは、ドラムの音しか鳴っていないとかはどう？

山田：それに編集でギターとベースが重なる。

古谷野：演奏してるとか（笑）？

Noguchi: Exactly. The way you hear the same sounds completely differently depends on how you open and close the door. But when this relationship becomes familiar, we can change the location of the speaker and film again—to disrupt one's sense of space.

Koyano: Maybe the same phrase can sound as if it was added during editing and separated from sounds in the film at first, but eventually turn into "sounds playing in the house" at some point. It would be interesting to use different editing and cutting styles for each phrase, like editing an image in sync with a phrase or cutting up sounds in sync with an image.

Noguchi: How about if we play only drum sounds from the speaker?

Yamada: ... And overlay guitar and bass sounds during editing?

Koyano: ... Or, if we play the guitar and bass on the scene? (laughs.)

Okada: Speaking of which, I was first thinking of asking all of you to play live in this house (laughs.)

Noguchi: Your neighbors would get upset for sure.

Okada: We would have to apologize to them in advance (laugh.)

PRODUCTION MEETING

岡田：そういえば、最初はここでみなさんに演奏してもらおうと思ってたんですよ（笑）。

野口：絶対怒られますよ。

岡田：近所にあらかじめ謝っておかなければいけないですね（笑）。

野口：とりあえず、ちゃんとしたフレーズじゃなくても、ありものの曲で、今日話に出た「スピーカーを置いて撮る」というアイデアを実験してもらうのがいいでしょうか。
次回はその映像を見ながら、編集上使えるネタについて話しましょう。

岡田：そうですね。みなさんの音楽を私がスピーカーで鳴らして撮って、それを見てもらうみたいな感じですね。

古谷野：次回は飲みに行きたいですね（笑）。

一同：じゃあ次回は飲みながら（笑）。

Noguchi: Anyway, maybe you could test the idea of "placing a speaker from which music comes out on the scene and filming it", which we discussed today. I think you can use any existing music—not necessarily newly composed phrases, and we can watch the film and talk about ideas for sound editing next time.

Okada: Got it. I can play your music from the speaker, shoot it, and show all of you the film then.

Koyano: It would be nice to go for a drink next time (laughs.)

All: Good idea (laughs.)

第2回制作会議
2018年12月15日　四条烏丸近くの居酒屋にて

前回の会議を受けて岡田が制作したふたつの試作映像を観ながら……。

岡田：こちらは前回と素材は一緒ですが、またイチからつくりなおして、音楽（アルバム「空間現代2」より「誰か」）を乗せてみました。この曲を選んだ理由は、一番PVっぽくないからです。映像はすべて4秒毎に切ってつなげています。

野口：なるほど、でもリズムが流れ出してからだとやはりPVっぽくなってしまいますね。最初のぶつ切りの感じの方がいいのかな。あと、お子さんのインパクトがすごくあるから、建築よりもお子さんを見たくなっちゃいますね。

岡田：そうですか（笑）？　最初は子どもをあまり入れてなかったんですが……。難しいですね。
もうひとつは、室内で曲を流しながら撮りました。
短いですが、後から編集で元の音源を一部重ねています。

野口：異質な音がふたつあるというのはおもしろいですね。

古谷野：前回も話に出ましたが、この建築は中と外というふたつの意味が錯綜している。映像にも、人のいる／いないや、綺麗な部分／日常で使っている部分、というようなふたつがある。
だからやはり音楽もふたつある、というのがいいかもしれませんね。

岡田：映像的には、今のところカメラを意識していない自然な感じですが、もう少し作為的に、たとえば子どもたちにセリフを言わせるとか、演じさせることもできるわけですが……。

Second Meeting
at a Japanese-style pub near Shijo Karasuma,
December 15, 2018

Viewing two sketch films made by Okada after the previous meeting.

Okada: This film is based on the same materials as the previous one, but I started over from scratch and incorporated music (a piece entitled "Dareka" from the album "Kukangendai 2") into it. I chose this piece because it sounds the least like a music video. The images are cut into 4-second segments and spliced together.

Noguchi: I see. But it still sounds like a music video once the rhythms kick in. I liked the abrupt cut-up feeling at the beginning better. Another thing is that your children left such a strong impression that I was drawn to them rather than the architecture themselves.

Okada: Really? (laughs.) I didn't really include them? in the film in the beginning... it's pretty difficult, isn't it...
For the other one, I shot some scenes while playing music inside the room. Although it's short, the original sound source is partially overlaid during editing.

Noguchi: It's interesting that there are two completely different kinds of sounds.

Koyano: As we spoke about previously, two meanings—the inside and outside—are intertwined in this architecture. The image also shows two opposing conditions, such as scenes with/without people, clean and neat/domestic and daily spaces and so on.
I think it would make sense to have two different kinds of music.

Okada: In terms of filming, people in the scenes are acting naturally and are not conscious of the presence of the camera for now. But we could perhaps have intentional scenes where, for example, the children could "act" and say some lines...

PRODUCTION MEETING

野口：そういうことよりも、たまに定点で撮るとか、こういう構造の建物に子どもがいて、こう使っている、というのがわかるカットを見たいと思いましたね。今回は「こういう建物の中で、人が生活するとこうなるんですよ」というのがおもしろいと思っているので、それがもう少し見えるシーンがあってもいい。
今の映像だと、家よりも、どうしても出来事を見てしまう。

古谷野：子どもが寝ているところを俯瞰したカットとかすごくいいなって気がしますよ。

野口：うん。だからもっと「そんなところで寝るんだ！」っていう感じが、もう少しわかりやすくなるといい。

岡田：建築の中でどこにいるのかがわかるって感じ？

野口：そうですね。われわれは実際にお邪魔したことがあるからだいぶ補完して見ることができましたが、そこをもう少しわかりやすく演出してあげた方が、より「なんでそこで寝るんだ？」というおもしろさが出る。
たとえばですけど、ソファが目立つシーンを外からガラス越しに撮って、「外からはこういうふうに見えちゃうんだ」と思わせた後に、ソファでお子さんが寝ている室内の俯瞰ショットを入れる。そうすると「あ、さっきのソファだ！ そこで寝ちゃうんだ！」となる、みたいな。
そういうカットの順序とか、ストーリーがあった方が建築に目が行くのかなと思いました。

古谷野：「あ、こういう漫画読んでるんだ」というように出来事に意識が行ってしまうのもおもしろいですが、それが構造にも見えるし、内容にも見えるという感じが出るとおもしろいと思います。

野口：中山さんの建築の「中と外」という概念が込み入っていることと、そういう住宅の中で岡田さんたちが普通に生活しているということ。それらが、浮き彫りになるような作品に

Noguchi: Apart from that, I think it would be nice to see some images shot from a fixed point, or a cut showing how the children are situated in the structure or how they use the house. I think what's interesting about this film is that it communicates "what kind of life people are living in an architecture like this," so I think it would be nice to have more scenes like this.
As for the current film, I can't help focusing on "events" rather than the house itself.

Koyano: I thought that the cut showing the sleeping children from a bird's eye perspective was really impressive, wasn't it?

Noguchi: Yes. That's exactly why I think you should make it easier for viewers to understand the context... so they can see "the children sleeping in a place like that."

Okada: You mean it should communicate where in the architecture they are in?

Noguchi: That's right. We were able to understood it better because we actually visited your place. If you can make it easier to understand the context, the viewers would notice the unique aspects—like "Why are they sleeping there?!"
For example, you can film a scene from outside of the house to first show how the sofa in the house is completely visible from outside through the glass, and then you can show a bird's eye view of your children sleeping on the sofa in the house... and one would say, "Oh, that's the sofa... they sleep on!"
I thought such image sequence or a story would effectively direct viewers' attention to the architecture.

Koyano: Although it is fun to pay attention to what is happening thinking something like, "Oh, they are reading this type of manga", I think it would be more interesting for viewers to feel that it looks like a structure and a content at the same time.

Noguchi: There are two unique aspects to this film. One is that two meanings, namely "inside" and "outside", are intertwined in Nakayama's architecture. The other is the fact that the Okada family live an ordinary life in such architecture. I think the film

なると成功なのかなと思います。

岡田：確かに、そうかもしれない。今の映像だと、この家を知らない人が見ると建築の奇妙さが伝わらない。普通の暮らしや、普通に子どもが勝手にいろいろやっていることが、「変な所の中である」という感じが、映像に共通のものとしてあった方がいいかもしれないですね。

古谷野：映像の途中で、「こういう家なんだ」と思える瞬間が1回は訪れてもいいと思います。今の映像だと「何か変な家っぽいぞ」とは思うのだけど、腑に落ちる時間がない。たとえば建物を縦に切った断面が想像できるようなカットがあるとか。これまで見せてもらった映像には、外観がほとんどないですが、意識的に排除しているのですか？

岡田：撮ってはいるんですけど、あまりおもしろくないんです。

野口：みんな見たことあるからですかね。でもだからこそ逆手に取れる気もします。「まさかこの空間で子どもがバスケをしているとは！」という。そういうカットをあえて使うのはありな気がします。

古谷野：最近「ヘレディタリー」（2018、アメリカ）というホラー映画を観たのですが、家の外観を撮っていて、昼だったのが一瞬で夜になるシーンがある。それが何かおもしろいなと思って。定点だと思っていたのにずらされる感じというか。
今回も、ずっと4秒毎の映像をつないできたのに、いきなり1秒で変わるとか、どこかで裏切るところがあってもいいのかなと思います。

野口：建物を見ていたら夜になるというのは、これまで意識していなかった時間の移り目をいきなり見させられた、という衝撃。

would be a success if it clearly reveals the two aspects.

Okada: Yes, that's a good point. The current film doesn't really convey the strangeness of this house to people who don't know the house. Perhaps the scenes in this film should evoke the common feeling that these events, such as daily routines or the children's self-motivated activities, "take place in a strange place."

Koyano: It would be nice to include some moments in the film where the audience would get an overall grasp of this house at least once. The current film makes us feel that there is something strange about this house, but there isn't a moment when we can get a clear picture of it. You could probably show a cut indicating an overall section of the building. All the images you showed us so far don't seem to include exterior views of the house. Are you deliberately avoiding them?

Okada: Actually, I have filmed some exterior views but they are not that interesting.

Noguchi: Perhaps that's because we all have already seen the house...? Anyway, I think you could take advantage of that un-interestingness and use some cut that would surprise us... like, "how could the children manage to play basketball in a space like this?!"

Koyano: I recently watched a horror film called *Hereditary* (2018, USA) There was a scene showing an exterior view of a house during the day, which suddenly changed into a night view the next moment. I was somehow intrigued by that scene... perhaps because of the feeling of being caught off-guard when I least expected it.
As for the current film, I think you could betray the viewers' expectations by suddenly changing the rhythms of the 4-second image sequence into 1-second, for example.

Noguchi: I think the abrupt change from the day view to the night view of the house gave an impact of being exposed to the shift of time that viewers never expected.

PRODUCTION MEETING

山田：今の4秒ずつの映像は、まったく時間軸は関係なくつないでいるんですか？

岡田：はい、まったく関係ないです。ただあまり夜は入れないようにしています。なぜかというと、昼だといろいろな日、全然違う季節も、一応同じ時間の流れのように見えるからです。どこに日の区切りがあるのか、時間が経っているのか、カットの違いなのかがわからないという感じが出ます。
あと、夜になるといきなり場面転換になってしまうんですよね。そこに、ストーリー性や意図を感じてしまうことに対して少し違和感があるんです。
ただ、これまでの話から、意図を感じないように夜のシーンを使うこともできるかもしれないとも思いはじめています。
昼になったり朝になったり、夜になったりがまったく脈絡なく起こるという感じで。

古谷野：映像の「はじまりと終わり」はどのように考えていますか？

岡田：うーん。私はプロの映像作家ではないので、ちゃんとしたシークエンス、はじまりがあって終わりがある、というのが上手にはつくれないんじゃかなと思っています。
でもたとえば、今回なぜ最初にあのカット（p.71左）を選んだのかというと、観客を最初に裏切ろうと思ったからなんです。建築作品の映像を見に来ているのに、なんかごちゃごちゃしているカットからはじまる。「これから、いわゆる建築の映像じゃなくて、すごい汚いものを見せるよ」みたいな（笑）、一応マニフェストですね。

古谷野：なるほど。

岡田：そういうところからはじまって、さっき言っていたみたいに途中で「どういう建築なのか」というところにはしっかり答えてあげることが必要かもしれないですね。そして、もう1回裏切る。

野口：その方が逆に裏切りのパンチ力が増しますね。

Yamada: Are the 4-second images connected randomly regardless of time sequence?

Okada: Yes, they are in a totally random order. But I tried to avoid night scenes as much as possible, because day time seems to have the same consistent flow of time regardless of what day or season it is. It is hard to discern the boundary between days and makes one lose the sense of time, and disrupt the boundary between different cuts.
On the contrary, scenes completely change at night. I feel a bit uncomfortable about the fact that a "plot" or "intent" seems to stand out too much there.
But after this discussion, I am beginning to think maybe I can use the night scenes without making it appear too intentional.
Day, morning, and night could happen in a completely random order...

Koyano: Do you have any ideas about how to "begin" and "end" the film?

Okada: Well... since I am not a professional film maker, it would be difficult for me to compose a proper sequence with a proper beginning and end.
But the reason I decided to shoot the cut (see Photo p.71 left) for the opening scene was because I wanted to betray the viewers' expectations. The film begins with a cut of a cluttered place, even though most viewers expect to see a film about an architectural work. It is as if we are declaring, "We are going to show you something really messy!" (laughs.) It is our manifest.

Koyano: That's interesting.

Okada: I guess we could start from that, but probably need to think about better ways to communicate "what kind of architecture this house is." Then, we will catch them out of the blue once more.

Noguchi: That would definitely intensify the impact of catching them out of the blue.

古谷野：それこそスプリットにして、外観を入れてもいいのかな。

岡田：そういう裏切り方もいいですね。
いかにもドキュメンタリーみたいな、作為のない日常の映像の後に、すごく計画されて編集された複数画面の映像になるような。でも、昼は、前面ガラスの反射のせいで外から中が見えないから、断面っぽい映像は夜しか撮れないんです。

野口：外観を撮るということは、あえてみんなが見たい「目玉商品」を使うということにもなりますよね。

岡田：はい。でも確かに、正面から、風呂にも、キッチンにも、真ん中にも人がいる、みたいなカットが撮れたら、あの建築らしさは出るかもしれない。

古谷野：あと前面の道が見えるカットも、もう少し見たいなと思いました。歩いている人が見えるとか。

野口：あれはわかりやすいよね。やはりある意味ベタというか王道みたいなシークエンスも、もう少しつくってみるというのはありかもしれないですね。

古谷野：終わりのカットは何か考えていますか？

岡田：まだノーアイデアですね。どういう終わり方が正解なのか。
あと、少し別の話にはなりますが、2種類の映像をつくるというときに、「建築的な」映像の方は、部屋が片付いていた方がいいのか、汚いままがいいのかというのも悩みどころです。

野口：「O邸」のおもしろさは、「おしゃれで現代美術っぽいのに、人が住んでいる」という驚きにあるのではなくて、「え？ どうやって住むの？」と思わせるところだと思うので、家具などがあることは全然OKだと思います。
2種類の映像は、家具がある／ないではなくて、人がいる／いないでつくれるといいのかもしれませんね。まさかお子さん

Koyano: We could split the screen and include exterior views.

Okada: That's a nice way to surprise them too.
We can shoot some documentary-like, unintentional images of daily life, followed by very complicated split-screen images that are perfectly planned and edited.
The thing is, we can't see inside of the house from outside due to reflections in the glass, which means that we can only shoot the sectional views from outside at night.

Noguchi: I suppose that your decision to film exterior views is almost like displaying "featured products" everyone wants.

Okada: Yes... But actually, if we can shoot a sectional front view with people occupying everywhere from the bathroom to kitchen to the center of the house, it can probably communicate the unique characteristics of the architecture.

Koyano: In addition, I would like to see more cuts from inside toward the frontal road... perhaps showing people walking outside.

Noguchi: Yes, that would obviously show the uniqueness. I do think you could try making more sequences that are rather "cliché" or "classic."

Koyano: How about the last cut?

Okada: I have no ideas yet... I'm not sure how best to end it.
There's also something else. As I decided to shoot two types of images, I have to make a difficult decision as to whether I should tidy up the messy rooms or just leave them as they are before shooting "architectural" images.

Noguchi: I think it is absolutely fine to keep the furniture pieces as they are, because what is interesting about the *O house* is not the fact that "people live in such a stylish and contemporary art-like house" but its unique quality that makes people wonder "how could they live in an architecture like that?"
The two types of images may be differentiated by the presence/absence of people, instead of the presence/absence of furniture—because nobody would imagine how carefree and openly

PRODUCTION MEETING

があんなにのびのびと生活しているとは誰も思わないですし（笑）。

岡田：なるほど、そうですね。寝ているカットがなぜおもしろいかというと「あ、この建物でこんなに無防備になれるんだ」という意外性があるからですもんね（笑）。

古谷野：生々しい、何か見てはいけないものを見ている感覚になる。

野口：そうそうそう（笑）。あそこは、ホテルのラウンジというか、ほぼ公共空間じゃないですか。
そういう意味で、最後のカットは、最初の方に戻って、お子さんの寝ている姿、というのがいいんじゃないでしょうか？

古谷野：最後は痕跡だけが映っているという感じで、人がいない方がいいのかもしれない。

野口：確かにそっちの方がいいかもしれないね。寝ていた場所だけが映るという感じ。

古谷野：おもしろそうですね。

岡田：いやー、ありがとうございます。考えてみます。

山田：そうしたら次回はある程度の映像があって、それに合わせてこちらが音をつくるという感じですかね？

岡田：そうですね。次のバージョンをお渡しします！

your children live their lives there (laughs.)

Okada: I agree. I guess people are taken by surprise to see the cut of a sleeping children because they realize that "someone can be very open and carefree in this architecture." (laughs.)

Koyano: I almost feel as if I am seeing something really crude... something we are not supposed to see.

Noguchi: Yes, exactly (laughs.) The house is like a hotel lounge... or almost like a public space, isn't it?
In this sense, the last cut could go back to the scene of a sleeping children at the beginning.

Koyano: I think it would be better to show only the "traces" of people in the end, without their physical presence.

Noguchi: Yes, that sounds like a better idea. Showing only the place where the children were sleeping.

Koyano: Sounds great.

Okada: Wow, thank you for your ideas. I will think about them.

Yamada: I suppose you will have certain amount of film made before the next meeting so that we will be able to make music to go with it.

Okada: All right. I will send you the next version!

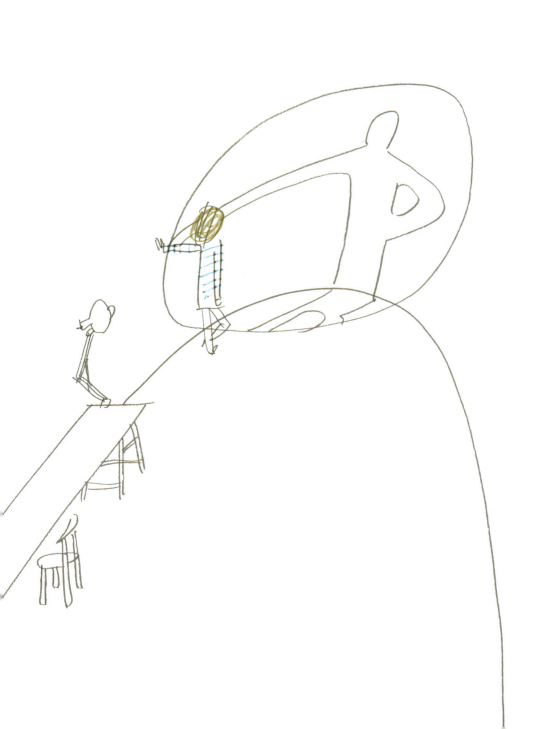

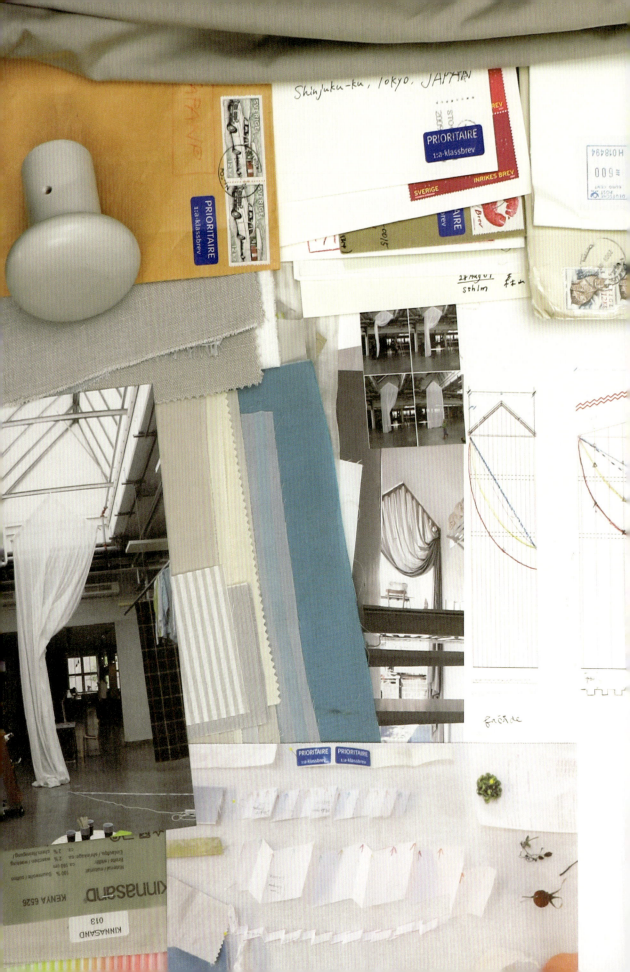

高さ7mのカーテン

北側立面に吊られた高さ7mのカーテンは、当時まだ学生であったテキスタイルデザイナーの森山 茜によって留学先のスウェーデンで制作された後、現場に持ち込まれたミシンで仕上げられた。
勾配屋根のため通常のレールを用いることができず、オペラカーテンの仕組みを応用した特殊な開閉機構が新たに開発された。幅2m、高さ7mの仕上がり寸法に対して、3倍ひだ、45㎡のKINNASAND社製コットンが用いられている。カーテン重量は30kgにも及ぶため、躯体に固定した19φのスチールパイプに28個のスナップボタンで吊られた。カーテンは建築と同様に、景観条例に沿った外壁同色。東京、ストックホルム間のやり取りのなかで、ドレスと撮影背景紙が同化したリチャード・アヴェドンの写真が、素材感の重要な手掛かりとなった。

7m Long Curtain

The 7m long curtain hanging along the north elevation was made by textile designer Akane Moriyama in Sweden where she had been studying as a student at that time. It was later brought to the site and sewn using a sewing machine there.
Because the curtain was to be attached to a ceiling under a pitched roof, we couldn't use standard rails. A special curtain operating system incorporating the mechanism of opera drapes was newly developed for this house. 45m² of cotton fabric made by KINNASAND was used to make a triple pleated curtain with a finished dimension of 2m (width) x 7m (height). The heavy curtain weighing 30kg hangs from a 19mm-diameter steel pipe fixed to the building frame using 28 pieces of snap fasteners.
The curtain is of the same color as the exterior wall conforming to the Landscape Act. While we exchanged ideas between Tokyo and Stockholm, a photo by Richard Avedon showing a woman's dress blending into the backdrop paper became an important reference image for materiality.

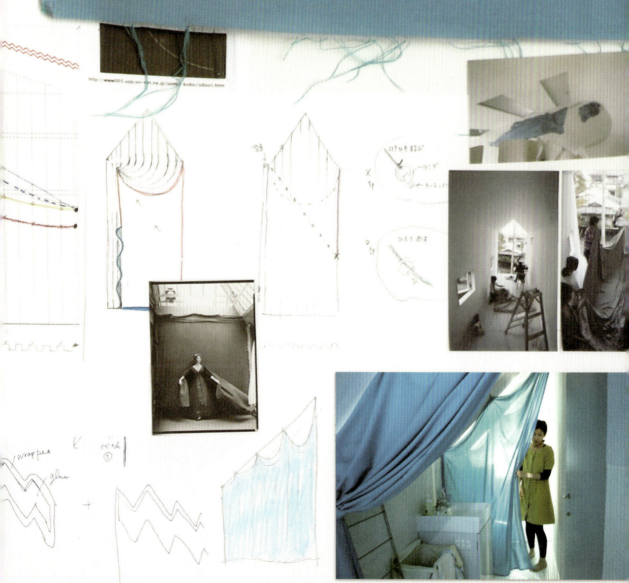

http://akanemoriyama.com

家の中と外を行き来する階段

通りから視覚的に連続した母屋の1階には当初から決められた機能はなく、寝室として使われる2階へ続く階段もこの場所の外側と結ばれている。母屋の外壁側は下屋の中まで同じ吹付け材が連続しているため、西側の下屋から2階に上る途中でこの外壁を通過して家の中に入ることになる。ひと連なりに見える階段は、工場で制作された4種類の異なる鉄骨階段の組み合わせで出来ている。形状が細かく変化する踏面は木製とし、外壁を吹付けた後に鉄骨フレームにボルト留めされた。

Stairs Going In and Out of the House

The first floor of the main building that is visually connected from the street doesn't have an initially designated function. Stairs leading to the second floor (used as a bedroom) is connected to outside of this place. The exterior wall of the main building and inside of the attached annex are seamlessly spray-coated with the same material. One enters from the annex on the west side and goes up along the exterior wall to go up to the second floor. The seemingly continuous stairs are actually composed of combinations of four types of different steel stairs. Threads in varying shapes are made of wood and bolted to the steel frame after the exterior wall was spray-coated.

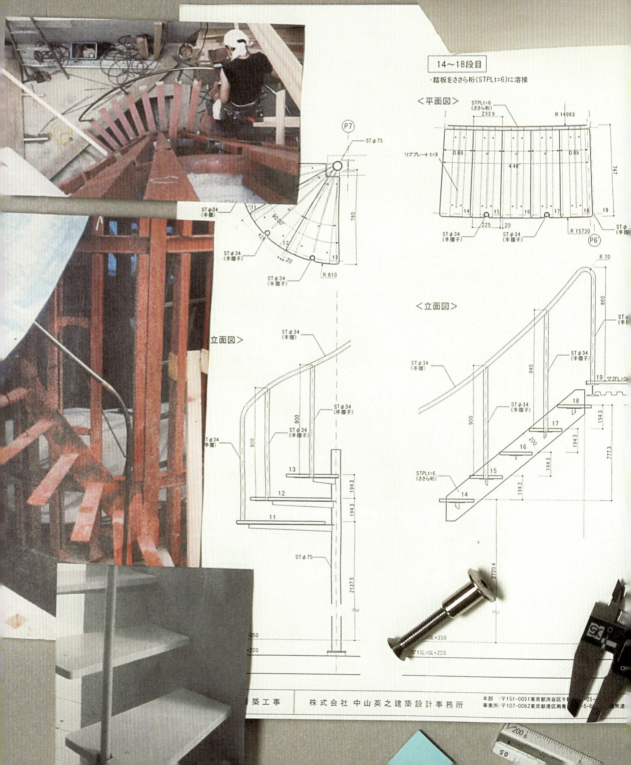

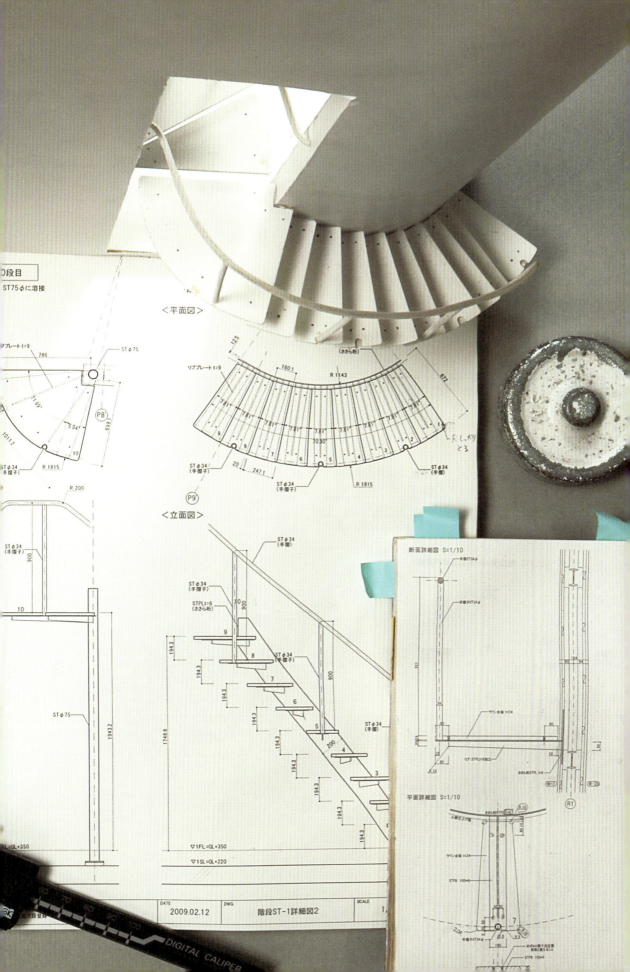

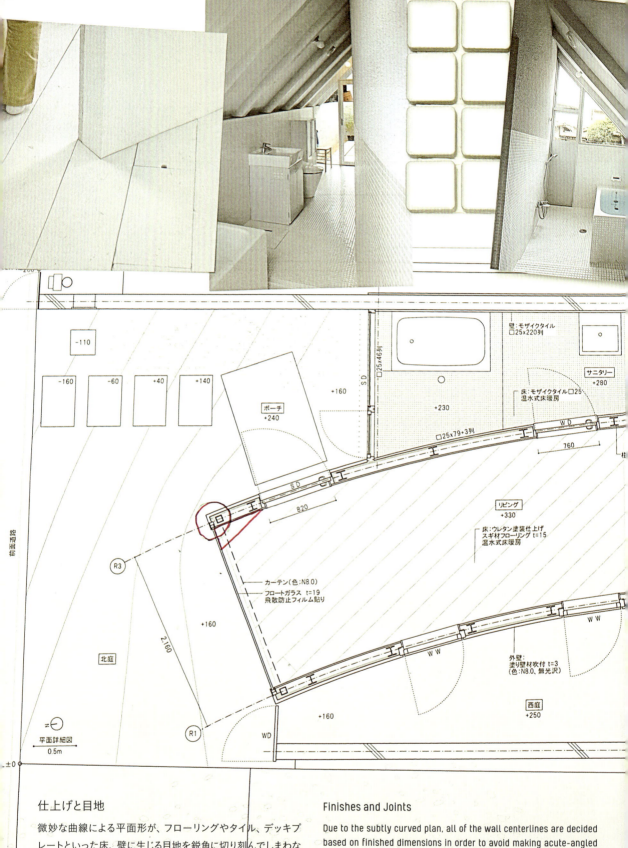

仕上げと目地

微妙な曲線による平面形が、フローリングやタイル、デッキプレートといった床、壁に生じる目地を鋭角に切り刻んでしまわないように、通り芯はすべて仕上げから逆算されて決められている。同じように見えるドアは、実際には奥に向かって徐々に扉幅とその間隔が小さくなり、実際よりも視覚的な奥行きが引き伸ばされている。

Finishes and Joints

Due to the subtly curved plan, all of the wall centerlines are decided based on finished dimensions in order to avoid making acute-angled cuts across joints of floor or wall finishes including floorboards, tiles, and deckings. All doors appear the same size, but the door width and the distance between the doors are in fact gradually reduced in order to visually enhance the sense of depth.

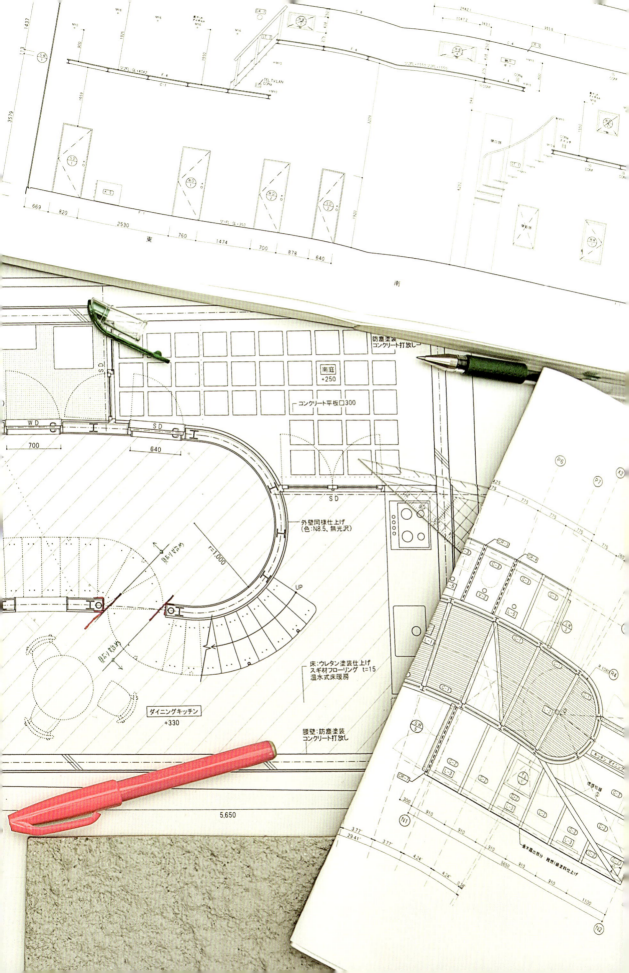

対談

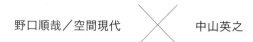

野口順哉／空間現代　　　　　中山英之

2018年10月4日、千鳥文化（大阪）にて
『中山英之｜1／1000000000』（LIXIL出版、2018）刊行記念イベントより

空間現代／野口：空間現代は、ギター、ベース、ドラムの3人で活動しているバンドです。東京で長く活動してきたのですが、2016年に京都へ拠点を移し、銀閣寺近くにライブハウス「外」という場所をつくりました。自分たちのスタジオとして使いつつ、ライブイベントも行っています。ライブハウスといっても普通と違い僕たちが企画したイベントだけを行う場所なので、毎日イベントをするわけではありません。その代わり、どれもすべておすすめできるものばかりです。知らないアーティストだけど来てみたらおもしろかった、と思ってもらえるような場所になればと考えています。

音楽活動をはじめて10年ほどになりますが、僕らはライブでやる曲が極端に少なくて（笑）。もともとつくるのが遅いということもあるのですが、東京にいた最後の1年はドラムの山田が大阪に転勤になってしまい、練習や作曲の時間がうまく取れなくなってしまいました。ライブ前日にスタジオで3時間ほど練習し、翌日に本番を迎えるというような状態が続き、新しい曲をつくれなくなっていました。でも、ライブのときに同じ曲ばかりやっていても、お客さんも、自分たちも飽きてしまう。限られた時間のなかで、新鮮な気持ちで演奏できる方法はないかと探し思い付

Round Table Talk:

Junya Noguchi/Kukangendai　　　　　Hideyuki Nakayama

Held at Chidori Bunka (Osaka), October 4, 2018
as part of a book launch of *Hideyuki Nakayama: 1/1000000000* (LIXIL Publishing, 2018)

Kukangendai/Noguchi: Kukangendai is a three-piece band with members on guitar, bass, and drums. We had been based in Tokyo for a long time, but relocated to Kyoto in 2016 and opened a live music joint called "Soto" near Ginkakuji Temple. We have live performances there while using it as our studio at the same time. Unlike most live music joints in general, we do not hold events on a daily basis, because we only hold events we organize on our own. For this reason, all of the events we offer are highly recommended. We want to create a place where you get to know artists you didn't know and have a good time.

It's been ten years since we started our band, but we actually have a very limited repertoire of pieces we can play for live performances... (laughs.) This is primarily because we take long time to make

TALK

いたのが、すでにつくった曲を一度分解して再度つなぎ合わせることで新しいフレーズをつくるというやり方です。あらかじめつくってある曲をいくつか詰め合わせるのがライブの基本的な考え方ですが、それを一旦やめてみました。30分間のライブなら30分でひとつの楽曲としても聞けるように再構成してみるのです。そうすればゼロから作曲するのではなく、今あるフレーズをどう料理するか、という方法に変わります。そうすると創作時間が少なくてもマンネリ化せずに新しいフレーズをつくり出せる。結構おもしろくて、それがだんだんと空間現代の音楽をつくる基本になっていきました。

だから音源を聴いたことのある人がライブを観ると、部分的には知っているフレーズがあっても、全体としては聞いたことがないものとして聞こえるのではないかと思います。

ライブって、自分の知っている曲が演奏されるとうれしくなりますよね。僕自身もそうですが、「次にドラムがバン！ と鳴るぞ……」とか、「このギターのリフが鳴ったら次に……」とか、自分の記憶と照らし合わせながら聴きますよね。あるいは、そうした観衆の予想を裏切る、上手なずらし方もあります。音源とはタイミングを少しずらしてみたり、サックスで演奏していた部分をキーボードでやってみたり。録音物とライブのあいだにほんの少しだけズレをつくっていく。ただ、僕たちはそんなに器用ではありません（笑）。そうして行き着いたのが、この手法だったのです。最近では「オルガン」という1時間の曲を制作しました。これは1時間でひとつのものをつくるというコンセプトでの最初の作品です。

ずいぶん苦労しましたが、結果的には自分たちであらすじのようなものをつくりながら進めることにしました。それは、テンションのグラフのようなものです。35分くらいでちょっと飽きるから、それくらいで手を変えてみようとか、ここで4つ打ちの単純なリズムを入れてみようとか、全体の設計図をつくりはじめました。「南国のリゾート」とか「バカンス」とか、謎の注釈を添えてみたり。そうして出来上がった設計図に当てはめていくように材料としてのフレーズをつくっていく、そういうやり方です。結構自信作なので、ぜひ聴いてみてください。

music, and secondly because Yamada (drums) had to relocate to Osaka for business during our last year in Tokyo and it became difficult for us to find time to practice and compose new pieces. We would practice only for three hours in the studio on the day before the show and perform the next day, and it was impossible to create new pieces. However, if we keep playing the same songs, both we and the audiences would get bored. We sought ways to play music with fresh minds when our time is limited and came up with a playing style where compose new phrases by "decomposing" and "recomposing" pieces we had made before. Basically, the musicians put together several pieces they had already made for live performances, but we decided to stop doing this for the time being. If our performance is 30 minutes long, we try to "recompose" a piece in such a way that one can listen to it as a 30-minute piece. In this way, our method switched from "composing from scratch" to "exploring ways to recompose phrases we have at hand." With this method, we can create new phrases within a limited time without getting stuck in a rut. It was quite enjoyable, and it eventually became a basic approach to creating Kukangendai's music.

When those who have listened to our original sound source come to our live concert, our music as a whole probably sounds to them like something they listened to for the first time, even if they recognize familiar phrases in some parts.

Audiences feel happy when a band plays a song they know. They listen to them play while comparing it with the song in their memory—speaking from my own experience—like, "After this phrase, the drum will go 'bang!' or "The guitar riff... and next comes..." Some musicians may skillfully defy audiences' expectations by playing with different timings than the original sound source, letting the keyboard play the phrase originally played by the saxophone, and so on. They can deliberately create slight

中山：空間現代の音楽のつくり方に、自分たちが生み出したばかりのものを、他人事のように素材として眺めてみるような感覚があるなんて、驚きました。実は僕たちの設計にも似たようなところがあるんです。

「2004」という最初の住宅でも、僕の描いた断片的なスケッチからスタッフが全体像を推理してつくった模型から設計がはじまっていたりするんです。

野口：たぶん、自分で考えた思考回路から逃れるというのが大事なのではないでしょうか。音楽をつくっているとき、妥当な正解には辿り着けるんですが、そこから外れたいという思いがあります。つまり、この旋律の次にバスドラムが4つ打ちで入ってくれば気持ちいいリズムになって、ノリやすくなるだろうということはわかるけれど、それだと紋切り型でつまらないと感じてしまう。まるで、何か見えない敵と闘っているような気分になってきますが、この段階を経ないと、おもしろいと思えるものにはならないと考えています。聴き手としてもつくり手としても、自分の想定する枠組みから外れてほしいと思うので。ただ、それは単に奇をてらうということではありません。中山さんのスケッチ、模型、出来上がった建築の写真を見ると、斬新な発想だなと思いますが、その一方で誰もが感じる居心地のよさや、ワクワクするものが根底にあると感じられ

---

deviations between the live performances and the original recording. Unfortunately, we are not skillful enough to do that (laughs) and so we finally came up with this method.
We recently composed a 1-hour piece called "Organ." This is our first piece created under the concept of "composing a piece in an hour."

It was a difficult process, but we decided to make some kind of "plot" as we proceeded. It was like a diagram indicating the level of concentration. We started making an overall plan, such as "change methods after 35 minutes when we get a little bored" or "insert simple quarter-note beats here"... while occasionally adding mysterious comments like "tropical resort" or "vacance." Then we made phrases or "materials" according to the overall plan we made. I think this piece is one of our best— please listen to it, if you have time!

Nakayama: I was surprised to hear the way Kukangendai makes music—or, your way of objectively looking at phrases you just made as "materials." In fact, we design in a similar way.

When we started designing *2004*, the first house we worked on, I handed my sketches showing fragments of my ideas to a staff member and he made a model based on the overall picture he imagined from my sketches.

Noguchi: It is probably important to get out of one's own pattern of thinking. When making music, I can find an appropriate answer, but I try to deviate from that. For example, I know that if I insert quar-

ます。子どもが寝転がって遊べる場所として、普遍的なよさがあります。今僕が写真を見て、素直にいいなあと思う、その感情こそが、中山さんの第一の狙いだということがよくわかります。普遍的なよさを求めることと、何かに闘いを挑むこと、それを両立できる人は少ないと思います。

中山：相手の見えない闘いと言われましたが、すでに自分たちのなかでセオリー化されたことの反復からは生まれない何かを探す過程というのは、本当に何と闘っているのかよくわからなくなってくるような、底の見えない恐怖だったりします（笑）。
「2004」で試した「断片的なスケッチによる設計」みたいな初めてのことも、それがスタイルとして形式化してしまうと、自分たちにもまだよくわかっていない何かを考え出していく方法にならなくなってしまって。
そこから「O邸」では、模型上の敷地に置いた景観法から決められた色と形の家型を、他人が置いたもののように扱ってみることをはじめた。そのまわりの余った敷地に、たとえば隣地からの木陰にキッチンとダイニングテーブルを置いてみたり、明るい道沿いにプール遊びのようにバスタブを置いたり。そのうちに家型がちょっと邪魔で丸められたり押されたりしていって、気付いたら生活に必要なものはぜんぶ家の外に並んでしまった。真ん中に残ったのは、自分ではあまりデザインしたつもりのない、変な形に歪んだ空っぽの家でした。

ter-note base drum beats after this melody, it would make danceable grooves—but I don't go with it because it's so cliché and boring. I feel as if I'm fighting an invisible enemy, but I think we can't create something interesting without this process. I want to stay out of my presupposed framework both as a listener and a composer. But it doesn't necessarily mean one needs to make something eccentric. Looking at your sketches, models, and photos of completed buildings, I feel you have very original ideas, but at the same time I can see that everyone feels the cozy atmosphere and joyous feelings underlying in your architecture. They are universally good places for kids to play and roll around. Looking at photos of your architectures now, I simply appreciate the goodness—and I understand very well that this simple feeling is something you seek more than anything else. Seeking the universal goodness. Challenging the unknown. I think very few people can do both at the same time.

Nakayama: You just talked about "fighting an invisible enemy." I feel that the process of seeking something that does not materialize from repeating practices we already theorized on our own is exactly like fighting something unknown—it gives me a bottomless fear (laughs.)
As for the method of designing from sketches of fragments that we used in *2004*, it worked at the beginning. But when it becomes stylized, it is no longer a method of creating something we don't know. In designing *O House*, we made a model of a basic house shape based on the color and shape designated by the Landscape Act, placed it on the site, and started treating it like something that someone else had left on the site. We put furniture on the empty ground around the house—placing a kitchen and dining table in the area under the shade of a neighbor's tree and a bathtub as if installing a mini-swimming pool in a sunny area along the road. Eventually, the shape of the house got in the way and began

何だかやっぱり、野口さんのお話とどことなく似ていますよね。空間現代では辿り着いた手法を理論化したりはしないんですか？

野口：2ndアルバム「空間現代2」に入っている曲のほとんどは、手法の発見のために試行錯誤するなかで完成しました。それをやりきって、「オルガン」や今つくっている3rdアルバムでは、その手法を〈手段〉として使っています。僕らなりの理論化と言えるかもしれません。

でも手法の発見における楽しさとそれを手段として使うことは全然違いますね。たとえば、お気に入りのちょっといいハサミを買ったとします。最初はハサミを使うこと自体、とても楽しいしうれしいと思うんです。使うこと自体が目的、というか。しかし、それが道具として定着すると、目的は別のところに生まれてきますよね。そうなると、買ったばかりのときに感じたおもしろさはなくなってしまう。それと同じことが、2ndアルバムをつくった後に起きたんです。

とはいえ、その手法は便利だから発想としては残っているし、自分たちの土台になっていますが、それありきでつくっていると、手垢にまみれたつまらない曲に思えてしまうんですよね。だか

to get pushed around and some of the corners got rounded, and all items of daily life were placed outside of the house before we knew it. What was left at the center was an empty house distorted into a strange shape.

It somehow resembles your story... Don't you ever theorize methods you've found?

Noguchi: Most pieces in our second album were completed while we struggled to discover new methods. After we managed to finish the album, we are using these methods as "means" to create the piece "Organ" and the third album in the making. Maybe that's our way of theorizing them.

But I think the joy we feel in the process of discovering methods and the feeling we get in using them as "means" are quite different.

Let's say we buy a pair of high-quality scissors that we like. At first, we really enjoy using the scissors—it is as if the act of using the scissors itself is the purpose. But once they become a familiar tool, the purpose changes. Then you no longer feel the fun you used to have when you just bought them. The same thing happened after we completed the second album.

Still, the methods remained in our ideas because they are convenient, and they still form the basis of our music. But if we take it for granted that we use them, the pieces we make somehow become so worn-out and boring. So, we struggled. We had to put ourselves in a situation where it was imperative that we utilized the methods as means for creation, instead of using them just because we wanted to. Perhaps this struggle may be a normal practice for other musicians, but we had never experienced it in the past. Maybe it is because we finally started to face our music. In this sense, we took on a new chal-

TALK

ら苦悩しました。その手法をやりたいからやっているだけというものではなくて、必然性があるからその手法を手段として採用する、という状態をつくらなければならない。ほかの音楽家の方にとっては当たり前のことかもしれませんが、自分たちにとってはこの状況は初めての事でした。ようやく音楽に向き合えるようになったということかもしれません。そうした意味で、今までの流れを踏襲しつつも、新しい事への挑戦として取り組んだのが、長編楽曲「オルガン」です。

中山：まだどこにもない手法をひとつ発見したことに対するよろこびは長続きしないのかもしれませんね。手法の発見はものをつくる原動力だから、いつまでも探し続けなければいけない。3rdアルバムは鬼門だとよく言われますが、どう展開していくのか、楽しみです。

野口：音楽を聴いたり、映画を観たりすると、感動するじゃないですか。当たり前ですが、その感動がやってくるものをつくりたい、という思いがあります。でも感動は直接つくれるものではありません。聴衆とつくり手のあいだには、作品や出来事があるだけです。感動の〈よりしろ〉になる可能性を追求するのが、ものをつくることの共通項なのかなと思っています。

中山：「感動」を直接差し出すことはできない、そうですよね。もちろん、期待された感動を上手に再現できる表現者もいるでしょうし、時にそれを「プロフェッショナル」と呼びもするのかもしれません。けれどやはり、感動を含む感情というのは、あなたにとってのこれがそうでしょう？　と差し出すものではなくて、その人の内から生じるものです。だからこそつくるときにも、一回自分自身を他人事のように眺めたり、自分以外の人間に解釈を委ねてみるような方法を選んでいるのかもしれません。

僕の場合それは、たとえば全体像のないスケッチを事務所の仲間に渡してみることだったし、空間現代にとっては、過去のフレーズを別の構成や文法に読み替えていくような方法だったのかもしれませんね。

lenge in using the same methods to create something new and conceived the long piece, "Organ."

Nakayama: I suppose the joy of discovering an unprecedented method doesn't last long. The discovery of new methods is a driving force in one's creative endeavors, which means that he/she has to keep exploring forever. People often say that the third album is a critical point in one's musical career. I am looking forward to your new development.

Noguchi: Audiences are moved by music or films. We naturally want to create something that moves them. But the experience of "being moved" cannot be created directly though. We and the audiences interact only through music and actions. We need to explore what moves people—I think that is a shared mission pursued by creators in all fields.

Nakayama: Such experience of "being moved" cannot be directly provided—I agree. Naturally, some creators are good at predicting and providing the kind of excitement or inspiration people expect—I think they are often called "professionals." But the experience of being moved is not something given by someone, but it naturally occurs in a person's mind. That's probably why I choose to look at myself objectively or ask someone else to interpret my ideas when I make something.

In my case, for example, I handed some sketches of bits and pieces without the whole picture to my colleague at the office. In Kukangendai's case, it was probably the method of reinterpreting and reconfiguring phrases you previously made into different compositions or syntax.

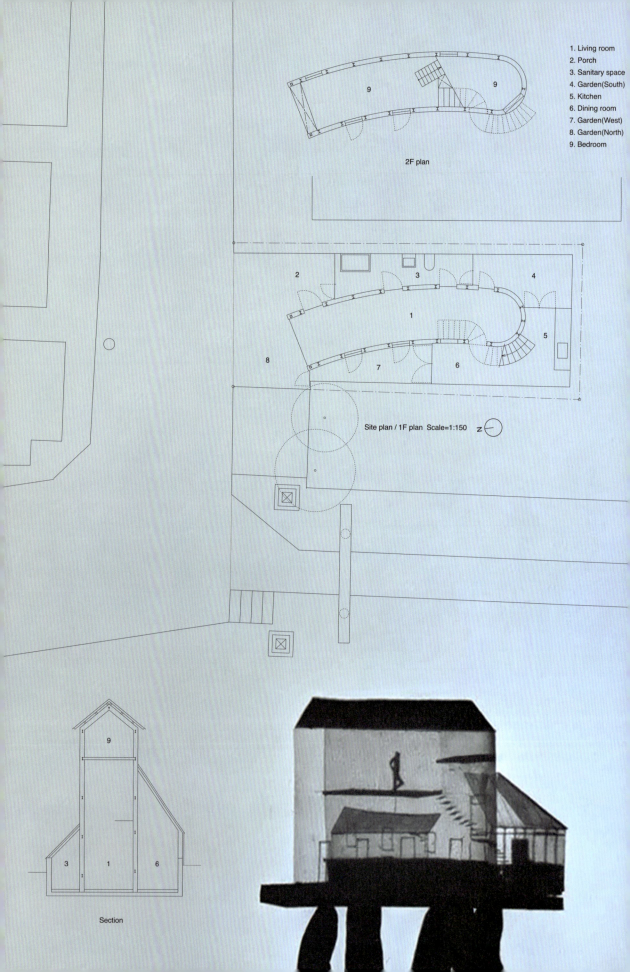

CREDITS

映画「岡田邸」

監督：岡田栄造、空間現代
音楽：空間現代
出演：岡田家
協力：松本花音

岡田栄造：京都工芸繊維大学教授、KYOTO Design Lab ラボラトリー長。デザインディレクターとしてグッドデザイン賞、Red Dot賞など受賞。編著書に『海外でデザインを仕事にする』（学芸出版社、2017）など。

空間現代：2006年結成、野口順哉（Gt、Vo）、古谷野慶輔（Ba）、山田英晶（Dr）によるスリーピースバンド。16年に活動の場を東京から京都へ移し、制作および公演拠点としてライブハウス「外」を開場。19年度京都市芸術文化特別奨励者。

書籍

写真・図版
森山 茜：p. 57、pp. 84-85（一部）
岡田栄造：pp. 60-63、pp. 68-79
松本花音：p. 64
岡本充男：p. 67（中央）
太田拓実：p. 67（右）、p. 88（右）
※上記以外は中山英之建築設計事務所

テキスト協力
出原日向子：pp. 90-95

建物「O邸」

所在地：京都府京都市
主要用途：専用住宅

設計：中山英之建築設計事務所（中山英之、三島香子）
構造設計：満田衛資構造計画研究所（満田衛資、柳室 純*）
*元所員

施工：志水工務店（永岡 弘）
カーテンデザイン・制作：森山 茜

敷地面積：83.33㎡
建築面積：42.90㎡
延床面積：59.71㎡
階数：地上2階
最高高さ：7,390mm
構造：鉄骨造
杭・基礎：直接基礎

設計期間：2007年5月 － 2009年2月
竣工：2009年10月

主な掲載誌、展覧会：
『GA HOUSES 113』、『新建築』2009年12月号、『Casa BRUTUS』2010年2月号、『MARK no.24』、「日本の家　1945年以降の建築と暮らし」展（2016年MAXXI国立21世紀美術館、2017年 バービカンセンター、東京国立近代美術館）

Film *Okada House*

Director: Eizo Okada, Kukangendai
Music: Kukangendai
Cast: Okada Family
Cooperation: Kanon Matsumoto

Eizo Okada: Professor of Kyoto Institute of Technology, Head of Kyoto Design Lab. Recived awards and prizes including the Good design award and the Red Dot Prize as a design director. Published "Kaigai de design wo shigoto ni suru" (Gakugei Publishing 2017).

Kukangendai: Kukangendai is a three-piece band by unya Noguchi (Gt, Vo), Keisuke Koyano (Ba), and Hideaki Yamada (Dr) started in 2006. In 2016, the band relocated from Tokyo to Kyoto and opened a live music joint "soto" as a base for their performance and music production. Selected as Kyoto City Special Artist for Promotion of Art and Culture 2019.

Book

Images
Akane Moriyama: p. 57, pp. 84-85 (some of the images)
Eizo Okada: pp. 60-63, pp. 68-79
Kanon Matsumoto: p. 64
Mitsuo Okamoto: p. 67 (center)
Takumi Ota: p. 67 (right), p. 88 (right)
Images not listed above: Hideyuki Nakayama Architecture

Cooperation
Hinako Izuhara: pp. 90-95 (texts)

Building *O house*

Location: Kyoto
Principal use: Private residence

Architects: Hideyuki Nakayama Architecture (Hideyuki Nakayama, Kyoko Mishima)
Structural consultants: Mitsuda Structural Consultants (Eisuke Mitsuda, Jun Yanagimuro*) * former staff member

General contractor: Shimizu-komuten Corporation (Hiroshi Nagaoka)
Curtain: Akane Moriyama

Site area: 83.33m²
Building area: 42.90m²
Total floor area: 59.71m²
Number of stories: 2 above-ground floors
Maximum height: 7,390mm
Structure: Steel frame (main structure)
Pile & foundation: Spread foundation

Design period: May 2007 - February 2009
Completion: October 2009

Publication and exhibition:
GA HOUSES 113, Shinkenchiku (December, 2009), *Casa BRUTUS* (February, 2010), *MARK* no.24, "The Japanese House : Architecture and Life after 1945" held at Barbican Centre in 2016, MAXXI, and the National Museum of Modern Art, Tokyo in 2017

Curves and Chords

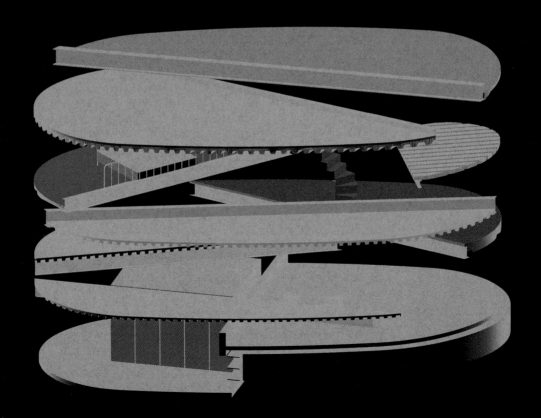

弦と弧

（2017年竣工）

Curves and Chords

〔Completed in 2017〕

監督　八方椎太
音楽　門田和峻

2階建てほどの大きさに、形のばらばらな10層の平面が重なった住居兼
仕事場。モーター制御された360度カメラが、高低差7.5mの吹き抜けを
上下します。ドールハウスを眺めるような視線の先を、ある1日の出来事
が淡々と流れてゆく、ただそれだけの映像です。何か特別なことが起こ
るわけではないけれど、移動したカメラが元の場所に戻ってくるたび、床
や、壁や、家具や、人の関係が、少しずつ変化して……。

Director: Shiita Happo
Music: Kazutaka Monden

It is a house and a studio consisting of ten layers of different-
shaped floor plates lying on top of each other within a volume
about the size of a two-story house. A motor-driven 360 degree
camera moves up and down repeatedly from the top to bottom of
the 7.5m high open space. The film simply depicts small things
that happened one day in this house as if looking inside a doll
house. Nothing special happens, but one eventually notices that
the relationships between floors, walls, furniture, and people
gradually change as the moving camera repeatedly moves back
to the same position.

Film

http://hideyukinakayama.com/cinema/04

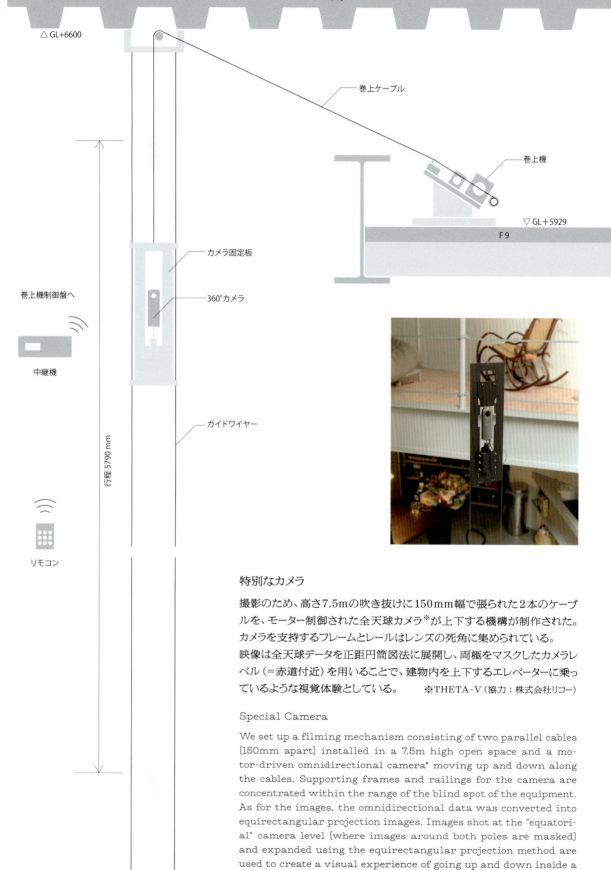

特別なカメラ

撮影のため、高さ7.5mの吹き抜けに150mm幅で張られた2本のケーブルを、モーター制御された全天球カメラ※が上下する機構が制作された。カメラを支持するフレームとレールはレンズの死角に集められている。
映像は全天球データを正距円筒図法に展開し、両極をマスクしたカメラレベル（＝赤道付近）を用いることで、建物内を上下するエレベーターに乗っているような視覚体験としている。　　※THETA-V（協力：株式会社リコー）

Special Camera

We set up a filming mechanism consisting of two parallel cables (150mm apart) installed in a 7.5m high open space and a motor-driven omnidirectional camera* moving up and down along the cables. Supporting frames and railings for the camera are concentrated within the range of the blind spot of the equipment. As for the images, the omnidirectional data was converted into equirectangular projection images. Images shot at the "equatorial" camera level (where images around both poles are masked) and expanded using the equirectangular projection method are used to create a visual experience of going up and down inside a building on an elevator.　　*THETA-V (Cooperation: Ricoh Co., Ltd.)

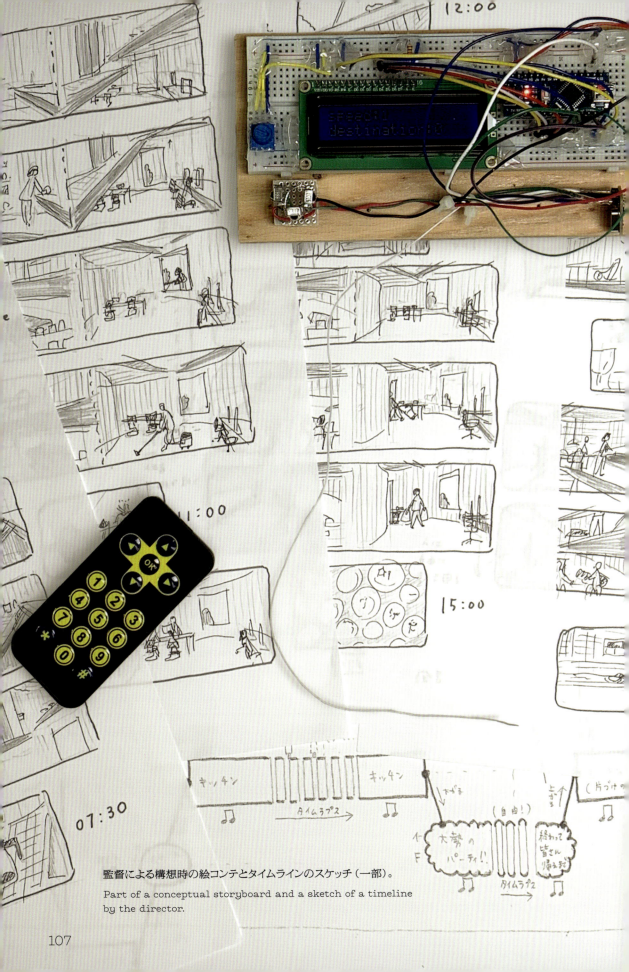

監督による構想時の絵コンテとタイムラインのスケッチ（一部）。
Part of a conceptual storyboard and a sketch of a timeline by the director.

ふたつの「リアル」

中山英之

映画の感想にしばしば言われる「リアル」という言葉がうまく使えません。「リアルな映画」と言ったとき、この言葉にふたつの意味が混ざっている感じがして、それが座りを悪くさせているのだと思います。「ジュラシック・パーク」[*1] の恐竜も「リアル」、ジュリエッタ・マシーナ[*2] の演技も「リアル」、どうもしっくりきません。たぶん、混ざっているのは「再現性」と「現実性」なのかな、と思います。そう友人に話したら、恐竜の方は「リアリティ」でいいけれど、もうひとつのモヤモヤした方は「アクチュアリティ」って言えばいいんだよ、と教えてくれました。なるほど。でも、「この映画はアクチュアルだ」なんて言うのも嫌味な感じがするし、僕は恐竜もジュリエッタ・マシーナも好きだから、「リアル」でまあよし、ということにします。

　ではなくて、せっかくだからリアルとアクチュアルの関係について少し考えてみたくなりました。映画が観られるようになったとき、「リアル」と「アクチュアル」には全然違いがなかったのではないかと思います。演出や演技が導入される以前なら、再現性と現実性も未分化だからです。「わざとらしい演技に興ざめした」みたいな感想は、そういう意味ではとても成熟しているのかもしれません。「リアリティのなさが、アクチュアリティを阻害していた」と述べていることになるからです。ところが、映画の感想はもっとずっと高度になっていきます。たとえば平気でこういうことが言われます。「CG表現ばかりが目に付いて、素直に感動できなかった。」これは大変です。言い換えるとこうなります。「リアリティの過剰な追求が、かえってアクチュアリティを阻害していた」。かと思えば、時にはこんなことを言ってみたりもします。「つくり話だとわかっているのに、どうして感動してしまうのだろう」。もう高度すぎます。「リアリティをあえて放棄することで浮かび上がるアクチュアリティ」みたいな感じでしょうか。僕たちはそれらをひっくるめて、単に「リアルだ／じゃない」と言っています。

建築の設計をしていると、つくりものと現実のあいだでいつもすごく悩みます。何度も手が入れられた古い農家にとても感動するのと同じようなことを、「設計」することができるのか。その悩みは、「アクチュアリティ」と「リアリティ」の関係についての悩み、と言ってみることができるかもしれません。そんな農家をリアルに再現したって、それがアクチュアルであるとは限らない。映画も似ています。

　たとえばヒッチコックは、いかにして観客を怖がらせるか、という意味で「リアリティ」と「アクチュアリティ」の一致を追求した作家なのだと思います。後に多くのヒッチコック好きがそのアイデアを解説したり応用したりしているので、僕みたいな素人でもヒッチコック映画を観ると、「映画」の定式が発明された瞬間に立ち会っているような気分になります。再現性と現実性の境界を忘れさせるアイデアの基礎をつくった監督、と言えるのかもしれません。でも実は、なぜだか逆のことがとても気になってしまう監督でもあります。たとえば「ロープ」[*3] という作品は、カメラを一度も止めずに撮った密室劇です。あらゆる意味で再現と現実の同化を図ったアイデアなのかもしれませんが、同時にヒッチコックの映画でもとりわけカメラの存在を意識してしまう作品です。当の監督を含めて、あまりいい評価を聞かない理由もそこにあるのかもしれませんが、それを言葉で表そうとすると少しややこしくなります。「リアリティ

*1
監督：スティーヴン・スピルバーグ／制作年：1993年／アメリカ
実在し得ない対象と世界の映像化、という今日のCGによる映画表現を決定的なものにした記念碑的作品。大半の恐竜はアニマトロニクス（機械制御されたフィギュア）によるものであったが、印象的なシーンにCGが効果的に用いられている。

*2
生没年：1921-1994／イタリア
「道」（1954）、「崖」（1955）、「カビリアの夜」（1957）など、夫でもあるフェデリコ・フェリーニ監督による映画作品の、リアリズムとファンタジーを同時に体現したような映画表現において欠くことのできない名女優。

*3
監督：アルフレッド・ヒッチコック／制作年：1948年／アメリカ
映画内で進む時間の進行と現実の時間を完全に一致させるため、撮影用フィルムの限界が10分程度であった時代に、さまざまなテクニックを駆使して全編カットなしの映画制作に挑んだ異色作。

Two Kinds of "Real"

Hideyuki Nakayama

People often use the word "real" to describe their impressions about films, but I find it difficult to use the word properly. I get confused when one says the film is "real," because the word can have two different meanings. They say that the dinosaurs in *Jurassic Park*[1] are "real," and Giulietta Masina's performance is also "real"—it doesn't sound quite right to me. I think it is because "recreatability" and "reality" are getting mixed up. When I told my friend so, he said that the dinosaurs can be understood as "reality" and the other case (more abstract kind of "real") as "actuality." That makes sense! But I will settle for using the word "real" for the dinosaurs and Giulietta Masina[2] (I like them both) for now, because it might sound a bit snobbish to say "this film is so actual."
Joking aside, I would like to delve into the relationship between "real" and "actual." I suppose that there was no clear distinction between "real" and "actual" when the cinema was invented. It is because "recreatability" and "reality" were probably not differentiated before creative direction and acting techniques were introduced to the cinema. In this sense, a comment such as "his unnatural acting was a real turnoff" perhaps indicates the audience's high level of maturity, because it means something like "the lack of reality hindered the pursuit of actuality." In fact, comments on films are becoming more and more elaborate. For example, someone may casually say, "I couldn't immerse myself in the film because the computer-generated effects really bothered me"—this is too advanced. It may be translated as "the overly intense pursuit of reality only hindered the pursuit of actuality." Or, someone else may say, "Why am I so moved by the film although I know it's a total fiction?"—this is beyond my comprehension. It perhaps means something like "the film dares to deviate from reality, and the intense actuality emerges as a result." We simply say that something is "real" or "not real", be it "reality" or "actuality."

When designing architecture, I struggle between fiction and reality. How can I "design" architecture offering impressive experiences similar to what people would experience in an old barn that had gone through multiple renovations? This struggle may be explained as a struggle between "actuality" and "reality." Even if I tried to realistically reproduce a barn like that, it would not be so "actual." I think the same applies to the cinema as well.
For example, I think Hitchcock struggled between "reality" and "actuality" with a focus on how to thrill the audience with suspense and terror. Because many Hitchcock enthusiasts and followers have written about his ideas or applied them in their films at a later time, even an amateur like myself is able to recognize the moments when basic formulas of the cinema were established when watching Hitchcock's films. We can say that he was a film director who created basic ideas on how to make people forget about the boundary between "recreatability" and "reality." On the other hand, however, I am actually intrigued by his completely opposite aspects. One of his films entitled *Rope*[3] was shot in one continuous take in a closed room. While this idea might have been an attempt to assimilate recreatability and reality in every way, I strongly sense the

---

[1]
Director: Steven Spielberg / 1993 / USA
This epoch-making film founded the basis of computer-generated animation visualizing virtual objects and worlds. For the most part, animatronic dinosaurs were used for filming, but computer-generated animation images are incorporated effectively in impressive scenes.

[2]
Born in 1921 and died in 1994 in Italy.
A great Italian actress indispensable for her husband Federico Fellini's film expression that simultaneously evokes fantasy and reality. She appeared in Fellini's films including *La Strada* (1954), *Il Bidone* (1955) and more.

[3]
Director: Alfred Hitchcock / 1948 / USA
A unconventional film completed in a single continuous shot in order to match the time in the film with real time. During this period, the longest possible duration of a single shot was ten minutes and it was made possible by making full use of various shooting techniques.

とアクチュアリティの一致を突き詰めたとき、むしろそれが映画であることのリアリティが増してしまった。」もっと単純に言い換えるとこうなります。「私は映画そのものを観た。」つまりこれは、もはや再現でも何でもないただの現実です。そして、それが一番「リアル」なのです。ヒッチコック映画を観ると僕は、監督はそれを通じて何か別のものを見せようとしているのではなくて、映画そのものをつくろうとしているんじゃないかとすら思うのです。

　今もその定式が応用され続けているというのに、当の発明主は定式それ自体が目的になってしまうことに冷静だった。そんなふうに想像してみたとき、では次に一体どんな映画を観ればよいのでしょうか。いっそのこと、それが「つくりもの」であることをあらかじめ観客に伝えてしまう映画はどうでしょう。主人公の進む先で通行人が歌い出し、雨すらタイミングを見計らって落ちてくる。フレッド・アステアやジーン・ケリーが踊り歌うミュージカル映画は、最初から再現としての「リアル」からほど遠い場所にあります。「リアル」と「アクチュアル」が映画の側であらかじめ分類済みなので、たとえば同じカメラの「長回し」でも、ヒッチコックとは趣が違います。映画「ザッツ・エンタテインメント」*4 のなかに、フレッド・アステアがほとんどアドリブにしか見えないような危ういダンスを、何テイクでも繰り返してみせるシーンがあります。リアリティとはまったく切り離されたところで、ダンスやオーケストラの現実性そのものが試されるのが、ミュージカル映画の気分のいいところです。だからこそ、それが暢気な戦意高揚映画であることとは別の場所で、ダンスやオーケストラはめいっぱいアクチュアルです。もうずいぶん前のことですが、この感じにとてもよく似た映画に出くわしました。「ポンヌフの恋人」*5 というその映画は、ミュージカル映画ふうのタイトルとは裏腹に、現代のパリを舞台に、そこに生きるホームレスを描いたドラマです。何を思ったか監督のレオス・カラックスは、パリの町並みをセーヌ川ごとそっくりそのまま屋外セットで「再現」してしまいました。ハトが飛び、はるか遠くに見えるビルのその先の交差点を曲がる車まですべてがキューで動いているけれど、単なる現代の風景なのでそのことには最後まで気付きません。映画セットの真骨頂は、一言で言えば超現実の再現です。この監督だって、その気になればパリを爆破するシーンも撮ってみせることもできた。でも、この作品では花火が上がるくらいで、最後までその壮大さを観客に打ち明けることなく映画は終わります。何てばかげた、と思います。でも同時にこんなふうにも思うのです。監督は、リアリティの追求をアクチュアリティと混同させる芸当として映画が採点されてしまうことから、映画そのものを救おうとしているのではないか、と。

同じような感じを受けたのが、ウェス・アンダーソンというアメリカの監督の映画「ライフ・アクアティック」*6 でした。謎の巨大鮫に仲間を奪われた船長の復讐劇、という設定なのですが、銃撃戦で急所を撃たれたはずの人間はけなげに傷口を押さえながら画面の隅に延々と見切れ続けて、結局そのままで映画は終わってしまいました。人の生き死にみたいな「リアリティ」の大前提からして、まったくでたらめな映画です。全編にわたって、台本、演出、装置、すべてがつくりものであることをこれでもか

*4
制作年：1974年（Ⅰ）、1976年（Ⅱ）、1993年（Ⅲ）／アメリカ
MGM制作のミュージカル映画群から名シーンや舞台裏を紹介する映画作品。パート3には、映画「ベル・オブ・ニューヨーク」(1952)でフレッド・アステアが「I Wanna Be A Dancing Man」を歌い踊るシーンと、衣装が地味という理由でNGになった別テイクの比較再生が収録されている。

*5
監督：レオス・カラックス／制作年：1991年／フランス
パリに実在する橋を舞台にした映画であるため、占有許可の問題から、撮影は南フランスの田園地帯に造成した人工池に組み上げた巨大なオープンセットで行われた。

*6
監督：ウェス・アンダーソン／制作年：2004年／アメリカ
映画の主要な舞台となる海洋生物調査船に、イタリアのチネチッタ撮影所に組まれた船全体の断面セットを用い、そうであることを隠さないカットを劇中に差し込むなど、映画という魅力的なつくり物への賛歌のようなシーンにあふれている。

presence of a camera in this film. This may be the reason why the film, including the director himself, was given little recognition, although it is difficult to explain it in words. We may be able to say that "an attempt to assimilate reality and actuality actually resulted in intensifying its reality as a film." Or, put it more simply, "We saw a film as it should be." In other words, this is just plain "reality" without reproduction—and it is ultimately "real." When I watch a film by Hitchcock, I can't help feeling that perhaps the film director's ultimate aim was to "make a film as it should be", rather than showing something else through a film.

I imagined that even though the "basic formulas" of the cinema have been repeatedly applied to film production even today, the person who established them was indifferent to using the formulas for their own sake. What sort of film shall we see next, then? We might as well watch a film that intentionally communicates its fictionality in advance. For example, imagine a scene where passers-by start to sing and the rain begins to fall perfectly in sync with the movement of a main character strolling along a street. Musical films featuring dances and songs by Fred Astaire or Gene Kelly are totally opposite of the "real." These films clearly distinguish between the "real" and the "actual", so "long shots" are used in completely different ways from Hitchcock's films. The film *That's Entertainment!*[4] features a scene where Fred Astaire repeatedly performs surreally acrobatic dance (looking as if being improvised on the spot) for multiple takes. What is refreshing about musical films is the fact that the "actuality" of a dance or an orchestra performance, totally detached from "reality", is are the main concern—dance and orchestra performances are truly "actual" in these films, no matter how carefree and high-spirited the stories may be. Long time ago, I came across a film that had the same sort of atmosphere as the films mentioned above. The film entitled *Les Amants du Pont-Neuf*[5] portrays a story of the homeless in Paris today, contrary to the sort of plots the musical-like title suggests. The film director Leos Carax, for some unknown reason, made an outdoor film set that perfectly recreated the Seine riverfront and the surrounding Paris urbanscape. Flying pigeons and everything else including cars turning a crossing past a building at a distance are moving according to the director's cues, but it looks like any typical contemporary urbanscape and the audiences don't notice that it is actually a set until the end. In short, the true worth of film sets is to recreate hyper-reality. Carax could have used the set to shoot a scene of Paris explosion if he wanted to, but nothing much happens except for some fireworks and the film ends without revealing the spectacular scale of the set. How absurd. But at the same time, it struck me that Carax was perhaps trying to save the film from being unjustly evaluated based on the general preconception that a film aiming to achieve the ultimate level of reproducibility simultaneously achieve a high level of "actuality."

I got the same impression from a film entitled *The Life Aquatic with Steve Zissou*[6] directed by an American film director Wes Anderson. It is a story of a captain who seeks revenge on a mysterious giant shark which ate his partner. One of the characters gets fatally shot during the gun

*4
Part 1: 1974 / Part 2: 1976 / Part 3: 1993 / USA
A film series introducing famous scenes and "behind-the-scenes" shots of musical films produced by MGM. Part 3 shows a comparison of an approved take of a scene where Fred Astaire performs "I Wanna Be A Dancing Man" and another take of the same scene which had been rejected because his costume was too plain.

*5
Director: Leos Carax / 1991 / France
The story takes place on Pont Neuf in Paris. Due to difficulties in obtaining permission for occupancy of the bridge, the film was shot on an open-air set in a rural area in the south of France, where they constructed a replica bridge over an extra-large artificial pond built for this occasion.

*6
Director: Wes Anderson / 2004 / USA
A section of a marine life research vessel, the main setting of the film, was constructed at Cineccitá studios in Italy. This film features various scenes celebrating the fascinating "artificiality" of film, including a scene revealing the entire set of the vessel placed inside the studio.

と白状し続ける映画という意味では、ミュージカル映画に似ているかもしれません。つまり、「映画の方が徹底してリアリティからの距離を示し続けてくれるおかげで、初めて生まれるアクチュアリティ」といった感じでしょうか。ただ、浮かび上がってくるアクチュアリティの質が、ミュージカルとはだいぶ違っています。それはたぶん、ヒッチコック監督も知っていた、映画そのものの中からしか出てこない、現実を超えた現実のようなものです。血のつながりすら超えた私たちにとっての「家族」という存在について、こんなにも胸を締め付けられるような切実さで問いかけてくる監督が同じ時代にいるから、僕はまた映画館に通ってしまうのです。

「弦と弧」という住宅で僕たちは、建築を、単に建築それそのものをつくるための言葉だけでつくってみようと決意しました。「ロープ」や「ライフ・アクアティック」のような、「映画という現実性」に導かれるように、僕たちも建築という建築をつくってみることに憧れたのです。建築家はつくりものしかつくれない。そのことに誠実でありたいという気持ちもあったのだと思います。

単位面積を最小限の周長で囲い取る丸い形の中に、1本の線を引く。ただそれだけの方法で、この住宅の構造体はつくられています。実際には建築は厚みのない線ではなくて、たとえば丸い形は外装材や構造体、断熱材や内装材といった複数の物質の重なりだし、1本の線には重力に釣り合った断面が生じます。丸と棒から生まれる弦と弧。幾何学とすら呼べないような単純な形でも、それが建築的な物質性を帯びると、私たちは実にさまざまな想像力を働かせはじめる。そこに空からの光が注ぐと、忘れていた野生がいつの間にか目を覚ます。そんなふうに僕たちは、建築がどこかにある現実の再現として採点されることから、建築を救おうとしている、と言ったら怒られてしまうかもしれません。でも、再現性としてのリアリティが、決して現実性としてのアクチュアリティに近づく方法ではないことを、つくりものしかつくれない建築家は証明してみせなければならないと、信じているのだと思います。

誰に頼まれたわけでもないこの勝手な使命感を前に心細くなったとき、僕の大好きな映画監督たちは「ほら、簡単じゃないか」と言って、それが「現実」として「実現」できるのだよと励ましてくれるのです。

初出：中山英之「映画についての映画について」（長島明夫＋結城秀勇 編『映画空間400選』pp.164-166、LIXIL出版、2011）を一部変更および加筆。

battle, and the dying man who is painfully pressing his hand against the wound somehow remains (although only partly shown) in the frame until the end of the film. This film completely ignores the major premise of "reality" such as life and death. It loudly confesses that everything—including the script, creative direction, film sets and more—is entirely "fictional" from start to finish, just like musical films. We could say that "the film successfully generates a sense of actuality for the first time as a result of its continuous effort to completely deviate from reality." The quality of "actuality" in this film is, however, largely different from "actuality" in musical films. What is shown here is something like a "hyper-reality"—a kind of reality only the cinema can recreate—that Hitchcock knew so well. Anderson poses us a question about the significance of "family" beyond blood ties in our time in such painfully moving and compelling ways. Film directors like him make me want to visit the cinema again and again.

Upon designing a house called *Curves and Chords*, we decided to create architecture using a purely "architectural" language. Inspired by the "actuality" of the cinema as exemplified in films such as *Rope* and *The Life Aquatic with Steve Zissou*, we felt compelled to create architecture for its own sake. Architects can create only fiction, and I wanted to stay true to that fact.

The structural frame of this house is simply composed of a round shape enclosing a unit floor area within the minimum perimeter and a line drawn inside. In reality, architecture is not composed of abstract lines without thickness. For example, a round shape consists of many materials including exterior finish materials, structural frames, thermal insulation, interior finish materials, and each line has a section designed based on gravitational loads. Curves and chords are composed of a circle and straight lines. Our imaginations are ignited when "shapes", even the ones too simple to be called "geometric shapes", are given architectural materiality. When the light pours onto them, our forgotten wild instinct in us awakens before we realize it. We may offend some people by saying that we are trying to prevent architecture from being evaluated for its ability to recreate certain reality existing somewhere this way. But we believe that architects—who can create only "fictions"—have to prove that recreating reality is not the only way to achieve actuality.

When I feel anxious about pursuing this self-assigned mission, my favorite film directors always encourage me by saying, "See, it's simple. You can 'realize' it as 'actuality'."

First published in: Hideyuki Nakayama "Eiga ni tsuiteno eiga nitsuite" (*Eiga Kukan 400 Sen* edited by Akio Nagashima+Hidetake Yuki, pp.164-166, Lixil Publishing, 2011). Partially revised.

上棟式の様子。鉄骨の梁(弦)に正対して敷かれた、コンクリート打設前のデッキプレート。

Framework completion ceremony. Steel deckings were installed perpendicular to the steel beams ("chords") before concrete casting.

設計検討時のスタディ模型。弦と弧がつくり出す形や、それらの立体的な関係を直感的に何度も描きなおすことのできる模型=道具が数多く制作された。最終模型の縮尺は1:20。

Study model made during the schematic design phase. We made many models (or tools) that allowed us to intuitively and repeatedly "redraw" shapes created by chords and curves and the three-dimensional relationships between them. The final model was made at the scale of 1:20.

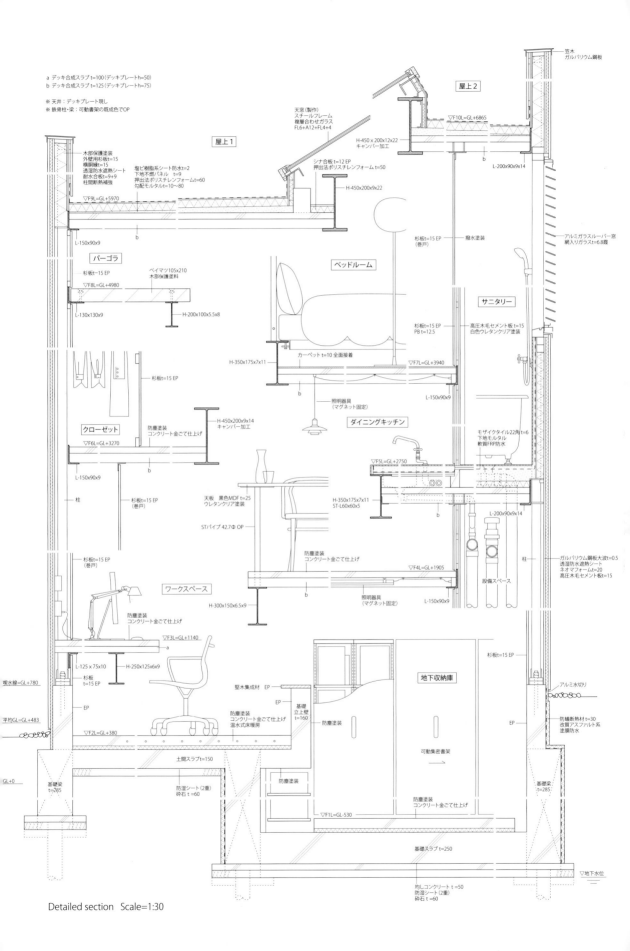

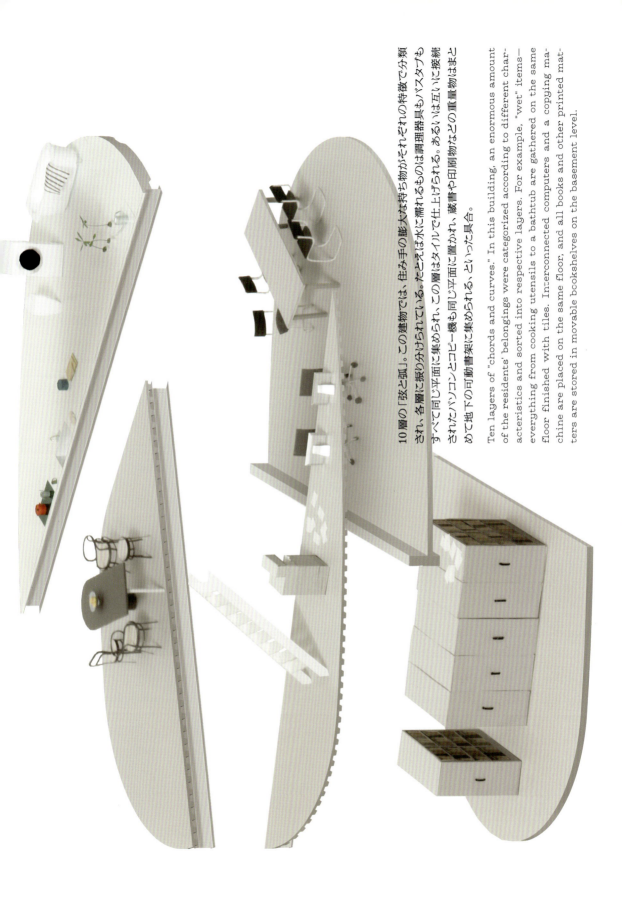

10層の「弦と弧」。この建物では、住み手の膨大な持ち物がそれぞれの特徴かで分類され、各層に振り分けられている。たとえば水に濡れるものは調理器具もバスタブもすべて同じ平面に集められ、この層はタイルで仕上げられる。あるいは互いに接続されたパソコンとコピー機も同じ平面に置かれ、蔵書や印刷物などの重量物はまとめて地下の可動書架に集められる、といった具合。

Ten layers of "chords and curves." In this building, an enormous amount of the residents' belongings were categorized according to different characteristics and sorted into respective layers. For example, "wet" items—everything from cooking utensils to a bathtub are gathered on the same floor finished with tiles. Interconnected computers and a copying machine are placed on the same floor; and all books and other printed matters are stored in movable bookshelves on the basement level.

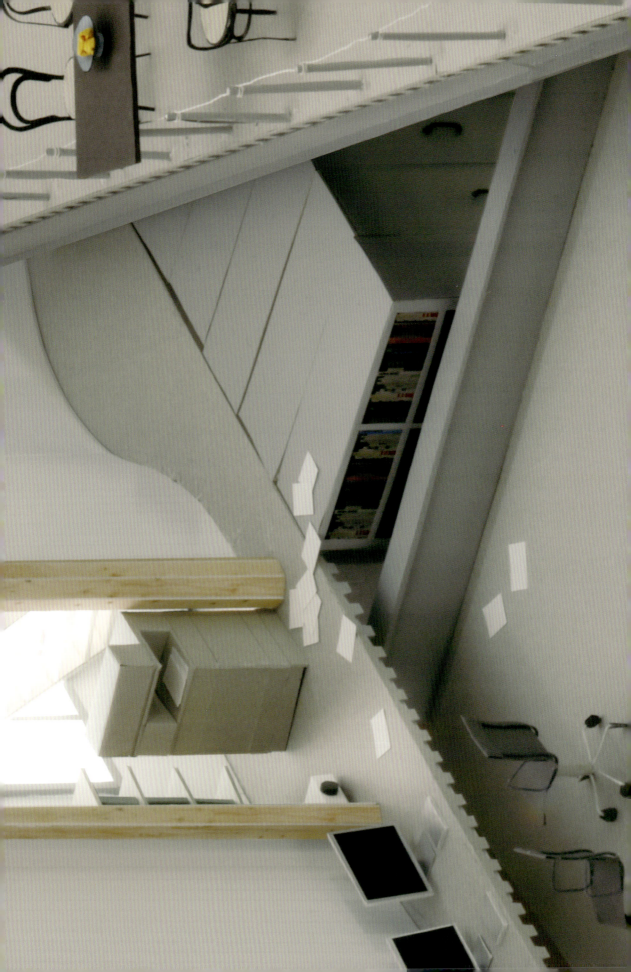

地下に置かれた既成品の可動書架は、ひとつ上の層から最上段の本が取り出せて、その天板はちょうどコピー機が置かれたさらに上の層にそろっている。このふたつの層のレベル差がちょうどデスクの高さであるために、パソコンはコピー機と同じ床に直に置かれることになり、そのまわりに散らばった資料は下の階に置かれた棚の上に広がる。

Prefabricated movable bookshelves are installed on the basement floor and one can reach for books on the top shelves from one level above. The top of the bookshelves are on the same level as the floor (two levels above the basement) where a copying machine is placed. Taking advantage of the fact that the height difference between the two levels is equal to the desk height, computers are placed on the same floor on which the copying machine is installed, and documents are scattered on the top of the shelves installed on the floor below.

タイル張りの層には、所どころに溝や窪みが設けられ、複数の排水口に向けて微かに配がつけられいて、その上にバスタブや洗濯機や鍋や食器が散らばっている。この場所は、ひとつ下の層から見るとキッチンになり、上に立つとサニタリーにも見える。

The tiled floor, which is gently inclined towards several drain holes, has grooves and depressions in some places, and a bathtub, a laundry machine, pots, tableware among others are scattered on top of it. This place becomes a kitchen when seen from the floor below, while it looks like a bathroom when one stands on the kitchen countertop and looks at it.

屋根にはふたつの層にガラスが架け渡されていて、室内から見上げると層の重なりの上にそのまま空が覗く。「部屋」と「屋根」という関係は消えて、この建築ではすべての場所が、地面と空のあいだの重なりの重なりの中に等価にある。

A glass roof spans across the two top floors, directing the view from the rooms below towards the sky through layers of different levels. The hierarchy between the "rooms" and the "roof" disappears: in this building, every place exists in equivalence among different layers between the ground and the sky.

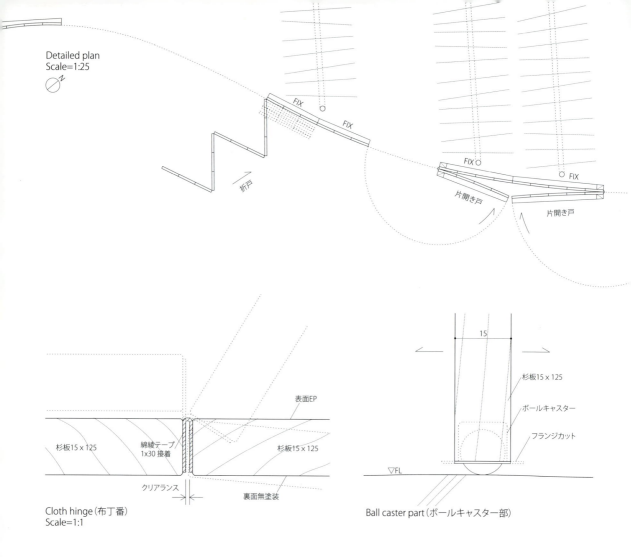

Detailed plan
Scale=1:25

Cloth hinge（布丁番）
Scale=1:1

Ball caster part（ボールキャスター部）

建物の室内側はすべて、白く塗った杉板が張られている。撮影スタジオのホリゾントのように奥行きが曖昧な空間に、形の違う「弦と弧」が浮かぶ。板と板の隙間に手を掛けると壁がするすると剥がれて、外壁の下地や柱や窓や、その向こうにある隣の家が現れる。この外壁と内壁のあいだの空間は所どころ膨らんで、洋服や階段や小さな部屋が隠れている。

All interior walls are finished with white-painted cedar wood board. Differently-shaped curves and chords float inside the space where a sense of depth is blurred as if being in a photo shooting studio with a cyclorama. When one puts his/her hand into the gap between the boards, the wall peels away and reveal wall substrates, columns, windows, and an adjacent house beyond. The gap between the exterior wall and the interior wall occasionally bulges out to conceal clothes, stairs, and small rooms.

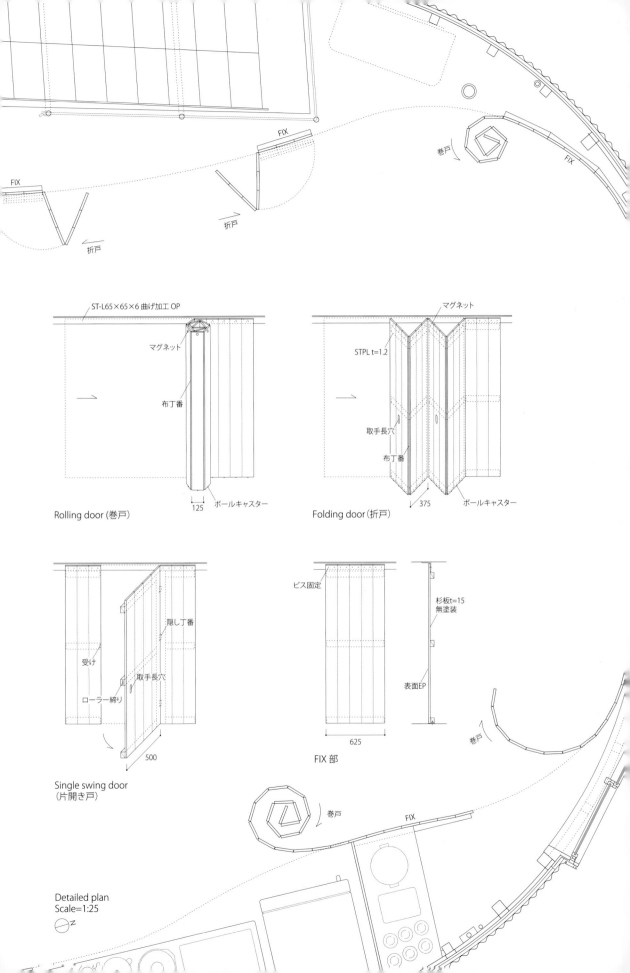

Rolling door (巻戸)

Folding door (折戸)

Single swing door (片開き戸)

FIX 部

Detailed plan
Scale=1:25

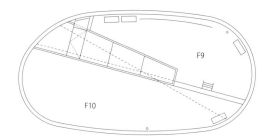

F9, F10 plan

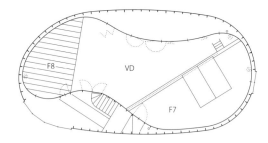

F7, F8 plan

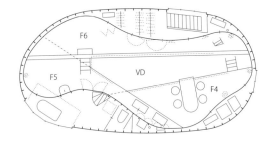

F4, F5, F6 plan

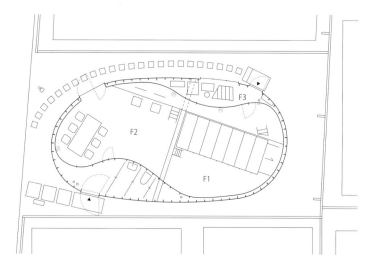

F1, F2, F3 plan   Scale=1:200

丸い形をした建物と敷地境界線のあいだには、元のままの土がそのまま露出している。いつの間にか伸びてきたケヤキやシソの葉やドクダミたちに混じって、発芽させたアボカドや贈り物のハーブが住まい手によって植えられて、それらがネックレスのように建物を取り巻いている。ポストや電気の引き込み用の電柱もそれらと一緒に並ぶ。

Existing soil is exposed between the round building and the site boundary. Among various trees and plants, including Japanese zelkova trees, perillas, and chameleon plants, germinated avocados and herbs given as gifts were planted by the residents and adorn the building like a necklace, accompanied by a post box and a lead-in pole.

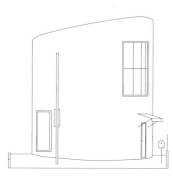

South elevation

128

映画「弦と弧」

監督：八方椎太　音楽：門田和峻　出演：施主とその友人たち
協力：株式会社リコー（撮影機材）、平田貴大（カメラ昇降装置）、矢口里菜子（チェロ演奏）

八方椎太：プロフィール非公開
門田和峻：作曲家。東京音楽大学卒業、東京学芸大学大学院修了。宗教学や神話などを元にした器楽・歌曲等の現代音楽作品の作曲・パフォーマンスを行う一方、映像音楽や舞台音楽も手掛ける。17年、久石 譲「Young Composer's Competition」にて「きれぎれ」(2017)が最優秀賞。

書籍

写真・図版クレジット
八方椎太（pp. 102-107）　谷口紅葉＋小林大陸＋中山英之（pp. 118-125）茂住勇至（p. 129）
※上記以外は中山英之建築設計事務所

建物

所在地：東京都　主要用途：事務所兼用住宅

設計：中山英之建築設計事務所
（中山英之、三島香子、藤瀬麻里*、松本巨志、山口紘奈*、堀部圭佑*）*元所員
構造設計：小西泰孝建築構造設計（小西泰孝、朝光拓也）
施工：深澤工務店（深澤正之、深澤伸行）

敷地面積：142.26㎡　建築面積：68.67㎡　延床面積：157.59㎡
階数：地下1階　地上2階　最高高さ：7,587mm
構造：鉄骨造　杭・基礎：鋼杭

設計期間：2011年9月-2014年6月　竣工：2017年3月
主な掲載誌：『新建築 住宅特集』2017年6月号、
『GA HOUSES 152』、
『Casa BRUTUS』2018年2月号

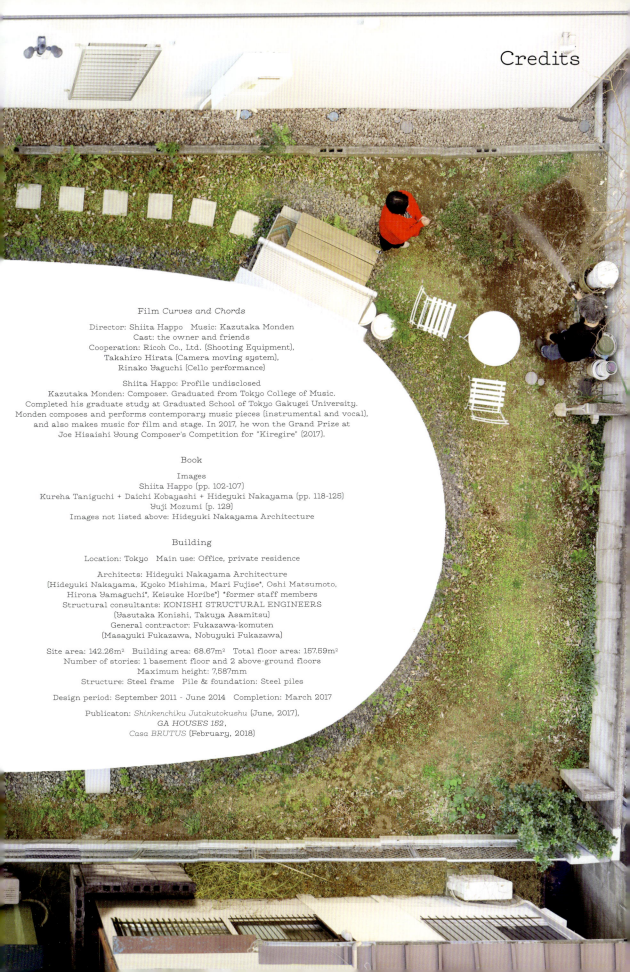

Credits

Film *Curves and Chords*

Director: Shiita Happo   Music: Kazutaka Monden
Cast: the owner and friends
Cooperation: Ricoh Co., Ltd. (Shooting Equipment),
Takahiro Hirata (Camera moving system),
Rinako Yaguchi (Cello performance)

Shiita Happo: Profile undisclosed
Kazutaka Monden: Composer. Graduated from Tokyo College of Music.
Completed his graduate study at Graduated School of Tokyo Gakugei University.
Monden composes and performs contemporary music pieces (instrumental and vocal),
and also makes music for film and stage. In 2017, he won the Grand Prize at
Joe Hisaishi Young Composer's Competition for "Kiregire" (2017).

Book

Images
Shiita Happo (pp. 102-107)
Kureha Taniguchi + Daichi Kobayashi + Hideyuki Nakayama (pp. 118-125)
Yuji Mozumi (p. 129)
Images not listed above: Hideyuki Nakayama Architecture

Building

Location: Tokyo   Main use: Office, private residence

Architects: Hideyuki Nakayama Architecture
(Hideyuki Nakayama, Kyoko Mishima, Mari Fujise*, Oshi Matsumoto,
Hirona Yamaguchi*, Keisuke Horibe*) *former staff members
Structural consultants: KONISHI STRUCTURAL ENGINEERS
(Yasutaka Konishi, Takuya Asamitsu)
General contractor: Fukazawa-komuten
(Masayuki Fukazawa, Nobuyuki Fukazawa)

Site area: 142.26m²   Building area: 68.67m²   Total floor area: 157.59m²
Number of stories: 1 basement floor and 2 above-ground floors
Maximum height: 7,587mm
Structure: Steel frame   Pile & foundation: Steel piles

Design period: September 2011 - June 2014   Completion: March 2017

Publicaton: *Shinkenchiku Jutakutokushu* (June, 2017),
GA HOUSES 152,
Casa BRUTUS (February, 2018)

camera 1

Junko Nakayama & Sein Sakaguchi

♩ = 100

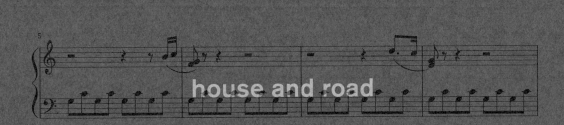

家と道
（2013年竣工）

House and Road
（Completed in 2013）

監督　坂口セイン

音楽　坂口セイン　中山順子

道を挟んで並んだ、素材は違うけれどまったく同じ形をした2軒の家。実はそれらは道の下でつながっていて……。4台のカメラで同時に撮影された生活の断片が、4曲のピアノ伴奏にあわせて繰り返し再生されるうち、少しずつ関係をもちはじめます。5周目で画面は4分割され、4重奏になったピアノとともに同時に再生されます。

Director: Sein Sakaguchi

Music: Sein Sakaguchi / Junko Nakayama

Two houses built out of different materials but with exactly the same shape stand next to each other across the road. They are actually connected under the road. Fragments of the family's daily life filmed simultaneously using four cameras gradually begin to connect with each other as they are replayed repeatedly along with the sounds of the piano playing four different pieces.

Film

http://hideyukinakayama.com/cinema/05

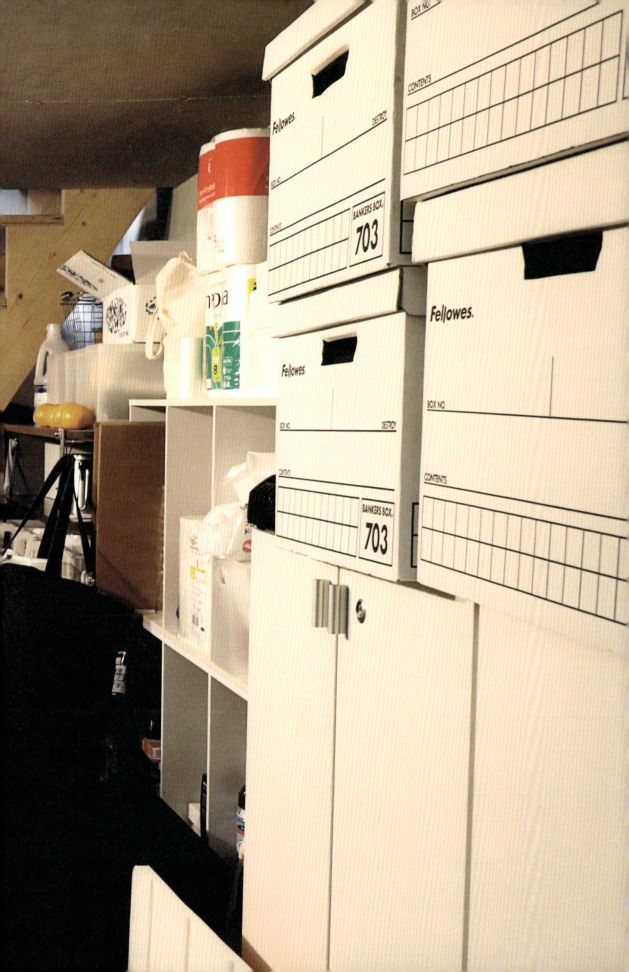

「家と道」によせて
坂口セイン

"気まぐれな道"をもつ少々変わったこの家は、私が中山事務所で働きはじめた当時、竣工が間近に迫っていて、仕上げのペンキ塗りを手伝ったのが最初の出会いだった。それから約5年、オランダ留学から帰国後、うれしいことに展覧会のための映像制作の話をもらい、それならぜひこの家を！と熱望した。

絵を描くことが大好きな夫婦のために建てられたこの家は、アトリエと住居の小さなふたつの建物から成り立っている。2棟のあいだには囲まれた中庭があって、大きな扉が開くとそこは突然道になる。小さな切り込みが入ったり消えたり、地図には記されていない通りが気まぐれに現れる。姿はとても控えめだけれど、ひときわ大胆でラディカルな性質をもつこの家にはどんなストーリーが内在するのか、その断片を覗いてみたいと思ったからだ。

しかし、夫婦の姿はもうそこにないという。完成からほどなくして、家は新しい主人を迎えたのだと聞き訪ねてみることになった。すると、そこには3人の可愛らしい家族が暮らしていて、どこか穏やかな"新しい"家の姿があった。それは、建築家が当初思い描いたものとは違うかもしれない。けれど、そんなことはどうでもよいことなのだと思うほど、家はそこにあることを祝福されて、毅然と存在しているように見えた。撮影の話をすると、僕たちでいいのならもちろんと、一家は笑顔で応えてくれた。

この映像は、ここでの家族3人の暮らしに、当初のコンセプトを少しだけ重ねたもうひとつのストーリーとなっている。過去と現在（今）が交差しながら展開していくストーリーは、4台のカメラで1カット同時撮影され、いくつものそこに「ある」と「あったかもしれない」家の風景を映し出している。

家族3人の何気ないやり取りをとらえるため、シナリオにはめいめいが通るルートだけを記して、あとは配達人を含む4人にお任せした。フレームの中と外を行き来する登場人物たちは、ひとつの映像では把握できない空間と空間を縫い合わせ、ひとつ、またひとつとシーンが重なるごとに全体の形が頭の中に浮かび上がってくる、そんな映像を目指した。また、シナリオには描けない街の流れや音は、その日偶然レンズに写り込んだそれらがそのままストーリーの一部となっている。

大扉が開き、外の世界が流れ込む瞬間、通りに現れるモノたちは、Here（ここ）とEverywhere else（ここ以外）が曖昧につながっていくことを感じさせてくれる。そのずっと先の世界まで妄想をめぐらせながら、この作品を愉しんでもらえるとうれしい。

Introduction

Thoughts on *House and Road*
Sein Sakaguchi

I visited this somewhat strange house with an "unpredictable road" for the first time when I went there to help paint it to meet the construction deadline after joining Hideyuki Nakayama Architecture. Five years later, Hideyuki offered me an opportunity to make a film for his exhibition when I returned to Japan after studying abroad in Netherland. I accepted his offer with great joy and eagerly told him that I wanted to film this house.

The house, built for a couple who loved to paint, consists of two small buildings, namely an atelier and a house. There is an enclosed courtyard between the two buildings which suddenly becomes a road when big doors open. This small "cut"—or a "road" not marked on the map appears and disappears unpredictably. Despite its smallness, this house is extremely bold and radical. I was curious to have a look inside, find out what kind of story exists there, and capture fragments of the story on the film.

However, I was told that the couple no longer live there. After hearing that a new owner took over the house shortly after its completion, I decided to pay a visit. There I found that a lovely family of three live in the house that somehow looked peaceful and "different" than before. It was perhaps not what the architect had originally intended. Nevertheless, the house stood there proudly and it seemed that its existence was celebrated by everyone, which made me think that it was totally fine for the house to be different from the original intention. I asked the family if I could film the house and they responded with a smile, "Of course, we would be happy to help."

This film combines the family's daily life with little bits of the original design concept to weave a new story. The story unfolds while alternating between the past and present (or "now.") The film, shot in one long take simultaneously with four cameras, depicts various scenes that "exist" or "might have existed" in the house.

In order to capture spontaneous interactions among the three family members, I indicated only which route each of them should take in the scenario and left the rest up to the four characters (the family and a delivery person.) I aimed to create a film in which the characters comes in and out of the frame while stitching together different spaces that cannot be grasped in a single image and an overall picture gradually emerges as viewers move through different scenes one by one. Flows and sounds in the city, which cannot be choreographed in advance, were captured on the spot by the cameras and incorporated into the story.

As soon as the big doors open and let the outside world flow inside, things on the street emerge and let us know that "here" and "everywhere else" are connected in ambiguous ways. I hope that audiences will enjoy this film while expanding their imaginations way beyond the house.

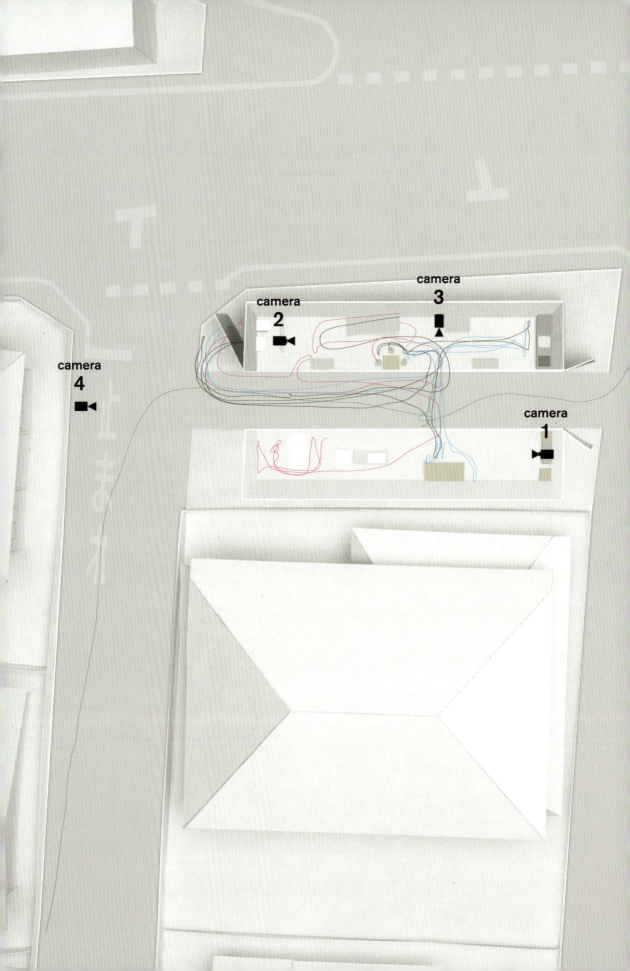

Cameras × Persons

4台の固定カメラと4人の人

窓の向こうに「道」が見えるカメラ、隣の「家」の窓の向こうにも同じ「道」が見えるカメラ、「家」から「道」越しに隣の「家」を覗くカメラ、その「道」にまっすぐに向けられたカメラ。
アトリエで作品制作を行う人、バスルームでリフレッシュする人、遊びまわる子ども、宅配サービスの男。

4 Fixed Cameras and 4 Persons

A camera looking out the window toward the road, a camera looking through the window in the adjacent house toward the same road, a camera peeking from inside the house into the adjacent house across the road, a camera directed toward the road.
A person making artwork in the atelier, a person refreshing herself in the bathroom, a child playing around, and a delivery man.

1

2

3

4

camera 2

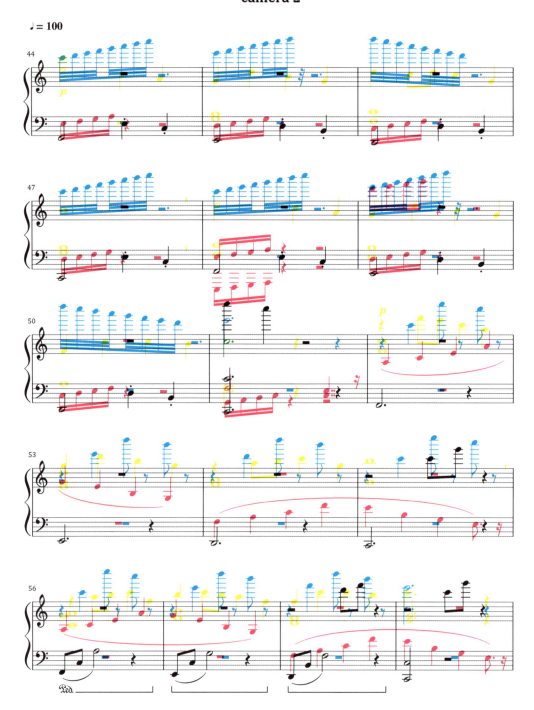

4本の映像のための4つのピアノ曲

リズムを刻む印刷機、トントンと階段を下りる人、ゆっくりと開く大きな扉、通りを行き交うバスや宅配便、カーテンの向こうから微かに水の音がする静寂なアトリエ。レンズにぱらぱらと写り込む、時に思いがけない人やモノ、空間一つひとつの仕草から思い浮かぶ音といくつかの旋律を、鍵盤で遊びながら、音源を送り合い創作していった。最後にすべてが重なるとき、家と街から流れるたくさんの音は4つのピアノと層になって小さな交響曲となる。――坂口セイン

Music

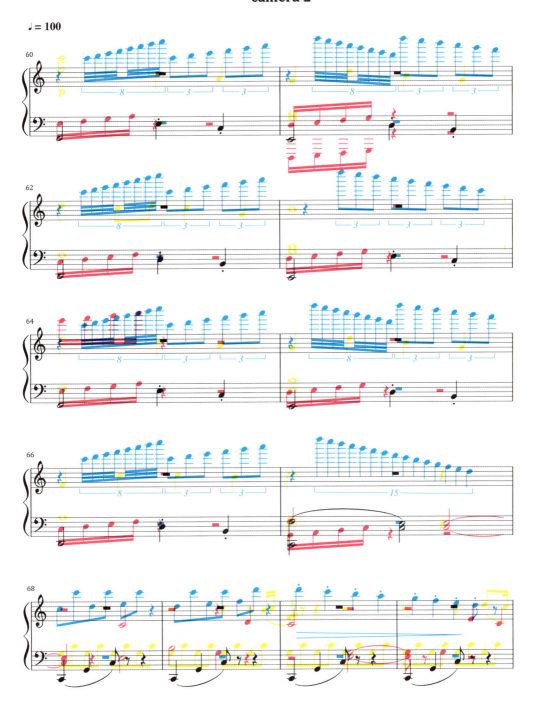

Four Piano Pieces for Four Films

A printing machine emitting rhythmic sounds, a person trotting down the stairs, big gates slowly opening, busses and delivery trucks come and go on the street, and a quiet atelier where subtle sounds of water are heard behind the curtains. We played with the keyboards, made some melodies inspired by movements of people, things, and spaces unexpectedly captured by the lens, exchanged sound sources, and gradually created the music. When everything came together, sounds from the house and the city were overlaid with four layers of piano sounds to create a small symphony. —— Sein Sakaguchi

宇宙の針穴　中山英之

ジル・ドゥルーズという哲学者に、その名も『シネマ』と題された大著があります。本の中でドゥルーズは、「ベルクソンの逆さ円錐」という思考モデルを用いて映画の歴史をたどります。この円錐とはどんなものなのか。

宇宙、つまりこの世の物質的なものすべてが編み込まれた織物のようなものに空けられた、小さな針穴を想像してみます。このピンホールを抜けた光はちょうどカメラ・オブスキュラの原理のごとく放射状に広がって、そのあいだのどこにスクリーンを置いても丸い映像を映し出します。ただしピンホールのすぐそばにスクリーンを差し込むと、映像は小さすぎて意味をなさない。では、無限遠に置かれた無限大のスクリーンには、一体どんな映像が映し出されるのでしょうか。ベルクソン／ドゥルーズによると、それはすべての記憶であるという。

宇宙というカメラ・オブスキュラの円錐に満たされている光は、あらゆる記憶である。そして映画を観るということは、自分なりの方法でこの円錐形の光の中に、そっとスクリーンを差し込んでみること……。ただし私たちのスクリーンは残念ながら、必ずしも平面ではありません。いつも静止しているわけではなくて、揺れ動くこともある。私たちが映画を観ることは、宇宙と記憶のあいだに波打ち、揺れるスクリーンを差し込む、そこにかろうじてとらえた光が脳の中に結んだ、小さな新しい記憶である、と。

宇宙にたとえられたものは、すべての物質的な世界です。では記憶とは何か。本の中でドゥルーズはそこに、映画の発明から、それが戦争のプロパガンダに利用された時代を抜けて、やがて映画に新しい波がもたらされる、その歴史を重ねます。私たちにとって映画を観ることは、そこに私たち自身のあらゆる記憶／歴史を見ようとすることに、似ているのかもしれません。

一本の映画が時に、その映画の中にある舞台や主人公たちの顛末を超えて、映画の外にある私たち自身の歴史を含む記憶に触れることがあるのなら、僕が建築をつくることも、どこかで宇宙という織物にピンホールを空けるようなものでありたい。そこにある生活がどこかで、自分たちを含むもっとずっと大きな記憶のスクリーンを、時々シートに腰かけて眺めるような時間に、つながっていてほしい。時々そんなことを考えます。

Pinhole in Space　Hideyuki Nakayama

Philosopher Gilles Deuleuze wrote a voluminous book entitled *Cinema*. In this book, he traces the history of cinema using a thinking model called "Bergson's inverted cone" as a reference. What is this "cone"?

Let us imagine a tiny pinhole in space—or something like a vast expanse of fabric interwoven with all physical entities. Light passes through the pinhole and radiates out on the same principle as the camera obscura, and if you insert a screen into the cone at any point, a circular image is projected onto it. When a screen is inserted too close to the pinhole, the projected image would be too small to see. Then what sort of image is projected onto an infinitely large screen placed at an infinite distance? According to Bergson and Deuleuze, it is an image of all memories.

Light filling the cone of the camera obscura through which we see space is all memories. And we see a "film" by quietly inserting a screen into this cone of light. Our screen, however, is not always a flat plane. It doesn't always stay still but sways sometimes. To see a film, we insert a gently swaying screen between space and memory—and a vague light captured on the screen creates a small and new memory in our brains.

Here, space represents the whole physical world. Then, what is memory? In this book, Deuleuze discusses memory in relation to the history of cinema from its invention, to the dark time during which it was used as a medium for war propaganda, and to new wave movements in cinema. When we go see a film, we are perhaps trying to see all our memories and histories.

If a film can convey something beyond the context and story of the characters and touch upon memories including our own history, I would like to make architecture as if making a pinhole in a fabric called space. Hopefully people living in the architecture I have designed have some time to sit down and see the large screen showing memories of all things including ourselves.

When I see the world we live in from a distance, I recall that when we learn drawing for the first time, a teacher would tell us, "Look at your drawing from a distance once in a while." When we draw, we alternate between looking deep within ourselves and looking

Essay

自分を含む世界を眺める。そういえば初めて絵を習うと必ず、「時々自分の絵を離れて見る」ように教えられます。だから絵を描く時間というのは、自分の内側を凝視することと、時々自分を外側から眺めることを、ひっきりなしに行き来することでもある。絵を描くことにとって、主観的であることと客観的であることは反対の概念ではなくて、ペアになって広がっていくはたらきです。

あるところに、同じアパートに部屋をふたつ借りている共働きの夫婦がいました。ひとつは住むため、もうひとつは趣味のための部屋です。ふたりの趣味は絵を描くことで、片方の部屋で心ゆくまま絵の具まみれになるのが、彼らの正しい週末の過ごし方でした。借りた部屋を汚さないように、絵を描くための部屋だけは内側がすべて透明なビニールで覆われていました。壁中に飛び散った絵の具がカンバスの輪郭を転写して、まるで反転した窓のように見えました。剥がしてビニールハウスをつくったら、きっと絵の具模様の壁にカンバス形に窓の空いた家が出来たでしょう。

この夫婦に家の設計を頼まれたとき、ビニールの部屋と住むための部屋をそのままの関係で敷地に置くことが、一番自然なことに思われました。別々の家を行き来するような関係は、アパートの時と同じです。違うのはこの家にとって絵から距離を置くことが、道を挟んだ隣の家の絵を見ることでもあるところです。実際、自分の絵から後ずさりすると、ドアを開けて外の道に出してしまうことになります。もっと下がると道を渡り隣の家のドアを抜けて、そこにあった食卓の椅子に腰かける羽目になる。クッキーでもつまみながら道越しに他人の家を覗くように自分の絵を見る。それは風景の中にいる自分自身の姿を外側から見てしまうことに似ていて——もしかしたら宇宙に空けたピンホールから眺める、私たちのあらゆる記憶？ と言ってしまうのは大げさかもしれませんが——世界をなるべく遠くから見ようとするときに、見ている世界の中に自分のこともちゃんと置いておく。この感じを、建築としてつくる方法について考える時間は、映画館のシートに腰掛けてスクリーンを眺める、その時間を思い浮かべることにどこか似ていると思うのです。

その後いろいろな事情が変化して、アトリエの透明な壁に絵の具が飛び散ることはありませんでした。代わりにその場所には活版印刷機が置かれて、工房を兼ねた住宅として使われています。

at ourselves from a distance. Subjectivity and objectivity are not necessarily opposite concepts when it comes to drawings, but they enhance one another and bring out new possibilities together.

There was a working couple who rented two apartments in the same apartment building. One was for daily life and the other was for their hobby, which was painting. They would spend perfect weekends there, just painting and covering themselves with paint as they wished. They covered the rented room entirely with transparent vinyl sheets in order to avoid messing up the walls and floor. Paint was spattered all over the vinyl sheet but we spotted some window-like blank squares at places where canvases had been hung. I imagined making a greenhouse using this vinyl sheet—a house with paint-spattered walls with canvas-shaped windows.

When they asked me to design their new house, I thought it would naturally make sense to place a vinyl-covered room and a room for daily life in the same way on the site. The rooms maintain the same relationship as in the apartment building: they would go back and forth between two different "houses" in the same way. But the difference is that they can look at their paintings from a distance—or from the other house across the path. For instance, if they keep stepping back from their paintings to take a look, they would eventually exit through a door, go across the path, enter a door of the other house, and end up seated on a dining table there. They would look at their paintings across the path as if peeking into their neighbor's window, while enjoying eating cookies. It is like looking at ourselves situated in some scenery from a distance, or (while it might be too much of a leap) looking at all of our memories through a pinhole in space. When we try to look at the world from the furthest point possible, we should keep in mind to place ourselves in the world we are looking at. In my view, thinking about a way to create this type of experience in architecture is somewhat similar to imagining the time when we are sitting in a cinema and watching a film.

Some changes were made later on, and no paint was spattered on transparent walls in the atelier after all. Instead of painting, they installed a letterpress printing machine there and the room is currently used as a workshop and a house.

Essay

151

2F

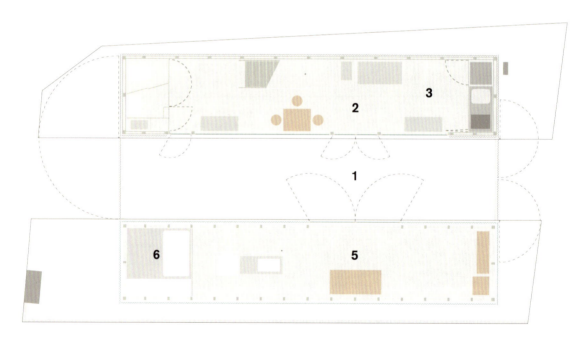

1F

Scale=1:100

Plan

3面接道の敷地に、仕上げの異なる同じ大きさ
の2棟の建物が、アスファルト仕上げの「道」と
同じ大きさの扉で、周辺道路と接続したり切り
離されたりする。

1. 道
2. リビング・ダイニング
3. キッチン
4. 寝室
5. アトリエ
6. 浴室

Two buildings of the same size but different
finishes are placed side by side with an asphalt-paved road inserted in-between on a
site facing the streets on three sides. The
"road" is connected and disconnected with
the surrounding roads by opening and clos-
ing the big doors of the same size as the
building elevation.

1. road
2. living/ dining room
3. kitchen
4. bedroom
5. atelier
6. bathroom

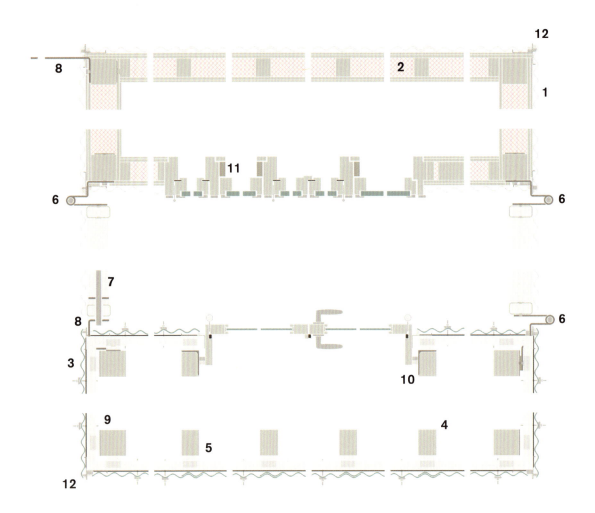

Scale=1:15

Detail

コンパクトな平面形に構造材が露出するため、寒暖の影響を受けにくく、アトリエ用途での釘打ちが容易な木造の軸組みが選ばれている。外壁の波板ピッチおよび重ね代から導かれた通り芯は、同時に敷地環境と大扉の軌跡に関係付けられている。

1. 小波スレート
2. 断熱材
3. 網入小波型ガラス
4. 木 105×75
5. 横銅縁 L40×40×3
6. 特殊SUS丁番
7. ロックピン
8. ロックピン受け
9. 補強 PL 4.5
10. 補強 L100×75×7
11. 補強 FB 60×25
12. コーナー水切り

Due to the compact floor plan with structural members exposed inside, wood frame construction was selected to protect the house against extreme temperatures and also to facilitate atelier activities such as nailing. The centerlines of columns were determined based on the flute pitch and the overlapping width of corrugated fiber cement slate boards used as an exterior finish and are also related to the site boundary lines and the traces of the movement of the big doors.

1. short-pitch corrugated slate
2. insulating material
3. wired short-pitch corrugated glass
4. wood 105×75
5. horizontal furring strip L40×40×3
6. custom made stainless steel hinge
7. lock pin
8. lock pin receiver
9. reinforcement PL 4.5
10. reinforcement L100×75×7
11. reinforcement FB 60×25
12. corner strainer

外装材には小波スレートと網入小波型ガラスが使用されている。波の寸法やピッチ、はたらき幅（重なる部分を除いた実際に見える部分の幅）、それらを留め付ける金物の配置がそろえられることで、2棟の建物は、並んだペアのようにも、ひとつの連続体のようにも感じられる。

Elevation

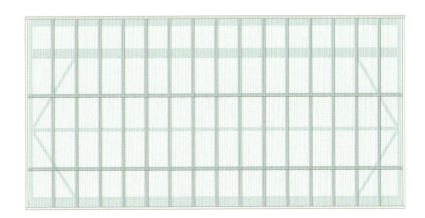

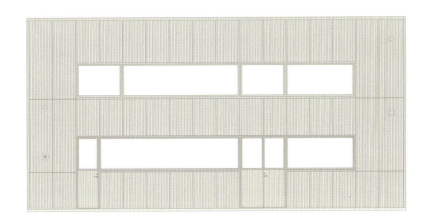

Short-pitched corrugated fiber cement slate boards and short-pitched corrugated wired glass were used as exterior finishes. By using the same flute pitch and height, the effective width, and positions of all metal fittings, the two buildings are sometimes perceived as a pair standing side by side and other times as a continuous body.

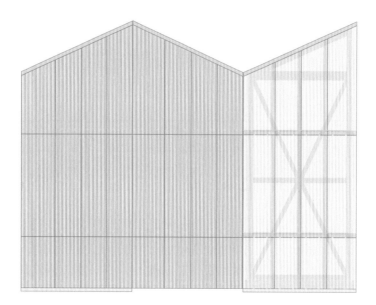

大扉は、開くと建物の妻側に重なる。ひとつの輪郭が崩れ、2棟のあいだに道が現れる。

Door

The big door, when opened, overlaps with the gable side facade of the building. A single outline of the facade is broken, and a road emerges between the two buildings.

Section

1. 道
2. リビング・ダイニング
3. 寝室
4. アトリエ
5. 倉庫

1. road
2. living/ dining room
3. bedroom
4. atelier
5. storage

大扉の使用マニュアル

100×50×6mmのスチール角パイプを用いたフレームに、外装材と同じ小波スレートが張られている。最大で幅2m×高さ5m、重さ400kgになる扉は、特注のステンレス製丁番により躯体に直接固定されている。扉に掛かる風荷重は1t近くにもなるため、丁番のほかにフランス落とし、かんぬき、戸当りなどが、使用マニュアルと併せて設計、制作された。

Use Manual for the Big Door

The frame is built out of 100×50×6mm steel square pipes and finished with short-pitched corrugated fiber cement slate board (the same exterior finish as the buildings). The 2m (width) by 5m (height at the highest point) door which weighs 400 kg, is fixed directly onto the building using custom-made stainless steel door hinges. Because the maximum wind load on the door is expected to be nearly 1 ton, the flush bolt, door bolt, and door stop in addition to door hinges were custom-designed and custom-made. A user manual for the door was also provided.

○各部位の名称と使い方

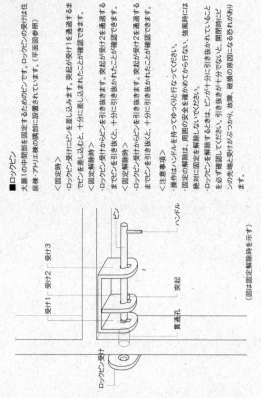

■ロックピン

大扉1の中間部を固定するためのピンです。ロックピンの受けは住居棟・アトリエ棟の壁部内に設置されています。(平面図参照)

〈固定時〉
ロックピン受けにピンを差し込みます。突起が受け1を通過するまでピンを差し込むと、十分に差し込まれたことが確認できます。

〈固定解除時〉
ロックピン受けからピンを引き抜きます。突起が受け2を通過するまでピンを引き抜くと、十分に引き抜かれたことが確認できます。
ロックピン受けからピンを引き抜きます。突起が受け2を通過するまでピンを引き抜くと、十分に引き抜かれたことが確認できます。

〈注意事項〉
操作はハンドルを持ってゆっくり行なってください。
絶対に固定を解除しないでください。
ロックピンを解除するときは、ピンがすっかり引き抜けていることを必ず確認してください。引き抜きが不十分だと、故障、破損の原因となります。開閉時にピンの先端が受けにぶつかり、故障、破損の原因になる恐れがあります。

■小扉

夜間・外出時・強風時のための出入口として、大扉2に設置されています。

〈中庭側から開ける時〉
開錠し、プッシュプレートを押して扉を開けます。

〈注意事項〉
小扉はゆっくり開閉してください。勢いよく開閉すると丁番・テーパーに大きな衝撃が加わり故障・破損の原因になります。
強風時には小扉が思わぬ風圧で勢いよく開くことがあるので、十分に注意してください。
サムターンは扉を開錠していれば建物の外周から手を入れて開錠することが可能ですので、最終的な保安を保障するものではありません。小扉を施錠する際には、防犯サムターンを取り付け、建物の施錠も併せて行なってください。

■フランス落し

大扉1、2、3に設置されています。フランス落しのつぼに差し込んで固定します(つぼの位置は平面図参照)。

〈固定時〉
突起が受け(上段)の切り欠きを通過するまでハンドルを回転させ、ピンをつぼに差し込みます。

〈固定解除時〉
ピンをつぼから引き抜きます。突起が受け(上段)を通過するまでハンドルを引き上げ、突起が受けから脱落しない位置にくるまでハンドルを回転させます。

〈注意事項〉
固定を解除する際は、必ず周囲の安全を十分に確かめ、ハンドルを持ってゆっくりと行なってください。
強風時には固定を絶対に解除しないでください。
風圧であっても、突風などにはピン受けが外れないように注意してください。
固定を解除する際にピン受けが外れるときは、突起が所定の位置にあることを必ず確認してください。ピンが上に引き上がらないと受けから落ちず、地面とピンの先端がぶつかり、破損の原因になります。

■戸当り

大扉が建物にぶつからないように、各大扉の下枠に戸当りが設置されています(戸当り受けの位置は平面図参照)。

〈注意事項〉
大扉はゆっくり開閉するようにしてください。扉を勢いよく戸当りにぶつけると大きな衝撃が加わり、大扉・丁番・戸当りの故障・破損の原因になります。ゴム・丁番の劣化やボルトの緩みがないか定期的に点検してください。
戸当りの先端にはゴムブロックがボルト止めで固定されています。
ゴムブロックの劣化やボルトの緩みがないか定期的に点検してください。

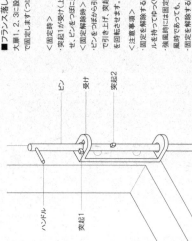

(図は固定解除時を示す)

○大扉の4つの開閉パターン

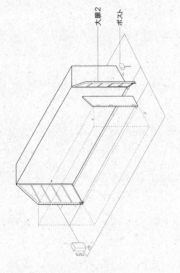

■すべての大扉を閉める。

夜間・外出時・強風時には、全ての大扉を閉め、出入りの際は小扉を使用してください。強風時には絶対に大扉の開閉をせずに、風が弱まるのを待ち、周囲の安全を十分に確かめてから開閉してください。

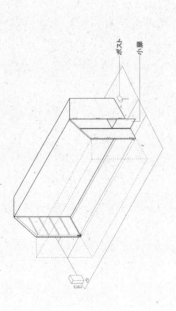

■大扉2を半開する。

中庭のプライバシーをある程度確保しながら、周囲の様子が感じられるように、大扉2を半開させて通用口として利用できます。部外者が中庭に立ち入る恐れがありますので、常に中庭に人の目が届くようにするなど、十分に注意してください。

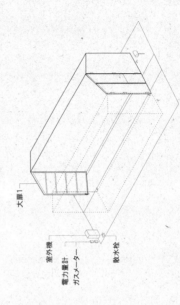

■すべての大扉を全開する。

すべての大扉を開けて、中庭を開放にして使用できます。部外者が容易に立ち入ることができる状態ですので、中庭に人の目が届くようにするなど、十分に注意してください。

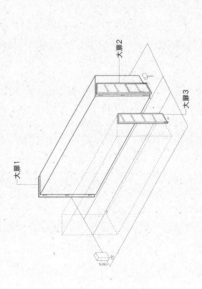

■大扉1を半開する。

各種メーターのチェックや散水栓の利用時には、大扉1を半開させて通用口として利用できます。ただし、大扉1はロックピンで固定されている状態が基本となりますので、短時間の開放に限定してください（大扉1の使用上の注意をご確認ください）

Credits

映画「家と道」

監督：坂口セイン
音楽：坂口セイン、中山順子
出演：千星一家、松本巨志
協力：千星一家、水本敦則、水本真規子、宮川 健、橋本吉史、平田貴大、ヨハンナ ビアンカ

坂口セイン：デザイナー。2010年西オーストラリア大学建築学科卒業。中山英之建築設計事務所勤務後、デザイン・アカデミー・アイントフォーフェン（オランダ）でデザインを学び、17年「studio sein sakaguchi」設立。

中山順子：鍼灸・あん摩マッサージ指圧師。2018年「アスナ鍼灸院」設立。

書籍

写真・図版
坂口セイン＋中山順子：表紙、p. 133、pp. 146-147
坂口セイン：pp. 136-141、p. 145
阿野太一：p. 151（コラージュベース写真）
※上記以外およびp. 151コラージュは中山英之建築設計事務所

参考図書
福尾 匠 著『眼がスクリーンになるとき――ゼロから読むドゥルーズ『シネマ』』（フィルムアート社、2018）

建物

所在地：東京都
主要用途：専用住宅

設計：中山英之建築設計事務所（中山英之、松本巨志、佐伯 徹*、堀部圭佑*、坂口セイン*、杉山幸一郎*、越賀香乃*）*元所員
構造設計：小西泰孝建築構造設計：小西泰孝、円酒 昂*）*元所員
施工：大原工務所（大原 彰、磯部弘太）

主なメーカー：北村鉄工所（特殊SUS丁番）、森の窓（木製建具）

敷地面積：105.16㎡
建築面積：39.60㎡
延床面積：59.99㎡
階数：地上2階
最高高さ：5,144mm
構造：木造
杭・基礎：ベタ基礎

設計期間：2010年12月 – 2012年10月
竣工：2013年6月

掲載誌：『GA HOUSES 120』

Film *House and Road*

Director: Sein Sakaguchi
Music: Sein Sakaguchi, Junko Nakayama
Cast: Chiboshi Family, Oshi Matsumoto
Coorperation: Chiboshi Family, Atsunori Mizumoto, Makiko Mizumoto, Takeshi Miyakawa, Yoshifumi Hashimoto, Takahiro Hirata, Johanna Bianca

Sein Sakaguchi: Designer. Graduated from The University of Western Australia in 2010. After working at Hideyuki Nakayama architecture, studied at Design Academy Eindhoven in the Netherlands. Established "studio sein sakaguchi" in 2017.

Junko Nakayama: Acupuncture / anma / siatsu practitioner. Established "Asuna acupuncture clinic" in 2018.

Book

Images
Sein Sakaguchi + Junko Nakayama: cover, p. 133, pp. 146-147
Sein Sakaguchi: pp. 136-141, p. 145
Daici Ano: p. 151 (photo use in collage)
Images not listed above and collage image (p. 151):
Hideyuki Nakayama Architecture

Reference
Takumi Fukuo *Me ga screen ni narutoki: Zero kara yomu Deleuze "Cinema"* (Film Art Inc., 2018)

Building

Location: Tokyo
Main use: Private residence

Architects: Hideyuki Nakayama Architecture (Hideyuki Nakayama, Oshi Matsumoto, Toru Saeki*, Keisuke Horibe*, Sein Sakaguchi*, Koichiro Sugiyama*, Kano Koshiga*) * former staff member
Structural consultants: Konishi Structural Engineers (Yasutaka Konishi, Noboru Enshu*) * former staff member
General contractor: O'hara Architectural and Construction (Akira Ohara, Hirota Isobe)

Manufactures: Kitamura Iron Works (custom-made SUS hinges), Mori No Mado (wood fitting)

Site area: 105.16m²
Building area: 39.60m²
Total floor area: 59.99m²
Number of stories: 2 above-ground floor
aximum height: 5,144mm
Structure: Wood
Pile & foundation: Raft foundation

Design period: December 2010 - October 2012
Completion: June 2013

Publication: *GA HOUSES 120*

Credits

英文翻訳：坂本和子

英文校正：織部晴崇

和文校正：株式会社鷗来堂

編集協力：江口宏志
　　　　　中山英之建築設計事務所 (三島香子、松本巨志)

English Translation: Kazuko Sakamoto

English Proofreading: Harutaka Oribe

Japanese Proofreading: OURAIDO K. K.

Editorial Collaboration: Hiroshi Eguchi
　　　　　　　　　　　　Hideyuki Nakayama Architecture (Kyoko Mishima, Oshi Matsumoto)

本書で紹介する5本の映画は、予告なくリンク先サイトでの公開を中止することが
ございます。あらかじめご了承ください。

Online viewing of the five films introduced in this book may be terminated
without notice. Thank you for your understanding.

5本の映画に関する問合せ先：中山英之建築設計事務所
For inquiries about the five films: Hideyuki Nakayama Archiecture
http://hideyukinakayama.com

中山英之

1972	福岡県生まれ
1998	東京藝術大学美術学部建築科卒業
2000	東京藝術大学大学院美術研究科建築専攻修士課程修了
2000-07	伊東豊雄建築設計事務所勤務
2007	中山英之建築設計事務所設立
2014-	東京藝術大学美術学部建築科准教授

主な作品

2006	2004｜住宅｜長野
2009	O邸｜住宅｜京都
	Yビル｜テナントビル｜東京
2012	Y邸｜住宅｜広島
2013	家と道｜住宅｜東京
	My Thread - New Dutch Design on Films DESIGNEAST 04｜会場構成｜大阪
2013-14	「クリスチャン・ボヌフォワ」展（銀座メゾン・エルメス）｜会場構成｜東京
2016	厲家菜 銀座｜レストラン内装｜東京
	石の島の石（瀬戸内国際芸術祭2016）｜公共トイレ｜香川
2017	弦と弧｜オフィス・住宅｜東京
2018	mitosaya薬草園蒸留所｜蒸留所｜千葉
	竹尾ペーパーショウ2018｜会場構成｜東京、大阪
2019	Printmaking Studio/ Frans Masereel Centrum｜
	アーティスト・イン・レジデンス｜ベルギー（LISTと協働）

主な受賞

2004	SD Review 2004 鹿島賞
2007	第23回吉岡賞
2014	D&AD賞
	Red Dot デザイン賞（最優秀賞）

主な著書

2010	『中山英之／スケッチング』（新宿書房）
2018	『中山英之｜1/1000000000』（LIXIL出版）

Profile

Hideyuki Nakayama

1972	Born in Fukuoka
1998	Graduated from Department of Architecture, Faculty of Fine Arts, Tokyo University of the Arts
2000	Master of Architecture, Graduate School of Fine Arts, Tokyo University of the Arts
2000-07	Worked at Toyo Ito & Associates, Architects
2007	Established Hideyuki Nakayama Architecture
2014-	Associate Professor, Department of Architecture, Faculty of Fine Arts, Tokyo University of the Arts

Works

2006	*2004*, Nagano, Japan
2009	*O House*, Kyoto, Japan
	Y Building, Tokyo, Japan
2012	*Y House*, Hiroshima, Japan
2013	*House and Road*, Tokyo, Japan
	My Thread - New Dutch Design on Films Exhibition, DESIGNEAST 04, Osaka, Japan
2013-14	*Christian Bonnefoi Exhibition*, Ginza Maison Hermès, Tokyo, Japan
2016	Chinese restaurant *Reikasai*, Tokyo, Japan
	Stone Island's Stone (ART SETOUCHI 2016), Shodo Island, Kagawa, Japan
2017	*Curves and Chords*, Tokyo, Japan
2018	*mitosaya botanical distillery*, Chiba, Japan
	takeo paper show 2018, Tokyo/Osaka, Japan
2019	*Printmaking Studio/ Frans Masereel Centrum*, Belgium (Cooperated with List)

Awards

2004	SD Review 2004 Kajima Prize
2007	The 23rd Yoshioka Award
2014	D&AD Award
	Red Dot Design Award (Best of the Best)

Books

2010	*Hideyuki Nakayama: Sketching/* Shinjuku Shobo
2018	*Hideyuki Nakayama: 1/1000000000/* LIXIL Publishing

建築のそれからにまつわる5本の映画

2019年5月22日　初版第1刷発行
2019年7月20日　初版第2刷発行

著者　中山英之
発行者　伊藤剛士
発行所　TOTO出版（TOTO株式会社）
　　　　〒107-0062
　　　　東京都港区南青山1-24-3　TOTO乃木坂ビル2F
　　　　［営業］TEL: 03-3402-7138
　　　　　　　　FAX: 03-3402-7187
　　　　［編集］TEL: 03-3497-1010
　　　　URL: https://jp.toto.com/publishing
デザイン　大島依提亜
印刷・製本　図書印刷株式会社

落丁本・乱丁本はお取り替えいたします。
本書の全部又は一部に対するコピー・スキャン・デジタル化等の無断複製
行為は、著作権法上での例外を除き禁じます。
本書を代行業者等の第三者に依頼してスキャンやデジタル化することは、
たとえ個人や家庭内での利用であっても著作権上認められておりません。
定価はカバーに表示してあります。

, and then: 5 films of 5 architectures

First published in Japan on May 22, 2019
Second published on July 20, 2019

Author　　Hideyuki Nakayama
Publisher　Takeshi Ito
　　　　　TOTO Publishing (TOTO LTD.)
　　　　　TOTO Nogizaka Bldg., 2F
　　　　　1-24-3 Minami-Aoyama, Minato-ku
　　　　　Tokyo 107-0062, Japan
　　　　　[Sales] Telephone: +81-3-3402-7138
　　　　　　　　　Facsimile: +81-3-3402-7187
　　　　　[Editorial] Telephone: +81-3-3497-1010
　　　　　URL: https://jp.toto.com/publishing
Designer　Idea Oshima
Printer　　Tosho Printing Co., LTD.

Except as permitted under copyright law, this book may not be
reproduced, in whole or in part, in any form or by any means,
including photocopying, scanning, digitizing, or otherwise, without
prior permission. Scanning or digitizing this book through a third
party, even for personal or home use, is also strictly prohibited.
The list price is indicated on the cover.

© 2019 Hideyuki Nakayama
Printed in Japan
ISBN978-4-88706-381-5